Sins of our Sisters

A MEMOIR

To Mary;
Blessings and Thank You!
Linda
July, 2019

Linda S. Mahlmeister

Cover design: John W Prince

Page design & typography: GoMyStory.com /John W Prince

Cover Photo: Andyworks/iStockPhoto

First Edition

Library of Congress Control Number 2019909467

Printed in the United States of America

Linda S. Mahlmeister

Sins of our Sisters

Memoir of a woman who was abused by a Roman Catholic Sister when she was a teenager and a young woman. Haunted by the abuse, she attempted to obtain acknowledgement and an apology from the Order, but was rebuffed by the leadership and shunned by some Sisters. A story of hurt, anger, depression and, ultimately, forgiveness.

ISBN 978-1-951188-00-9

'TRUTH TO POWER"
— Morning Joe

My Memoir is dedicated to all females who have been sexually abused, thus emotioinally and spiritually abused, by Religious Women, Nuns and Sisters.

———

"Act justly, love tenderly, and walk humbly with your God."
— Micah 6:8

———

Another brave soul to "truth to power"
— Dr. Christine Blasey Ford

TABLE OF CONTENTS

INTRODUCTION

For years I have kept journals where I wrote my thoughts and feelings, many of which focused on the fact that I was sexually abused by a Sister, Sister Rita Celine Weadick, a Sister of Charity of Cincinnati*, (SC). She was a Professed Religious, meaning a Canonically vowed person, supposed to be living out her life guided by her vows of Poverty, Chastity, and Obedience. (Her Congregation's Directives and the Roman Catholic Church dictate these vows.) This book is an expansion of my journals, but not a labor of love; for over sixty years, I have been in great emotional pain.

Despite my anguish, in order to move toward healing, I have decided to write and publish this book for several reasons. First, I was taught "The Truth Shall Set You Free." I am hoping to be set free from these dark memories.

Also, I write in hopes that the process will put an end to my anger

---

* There are a number of Sisters of Charity Congregations in the U.S. and Canada, each claiming Mother Seton as their foundress. This is why I am referring to the "Sisters of Charity of Cincinnati," to identify them from the other Sisters of Charity.

and rage about having my innocence stolen by a Sister's selfish and destructive seduction. I need to honor my lost innocence and youth by better understanding how an adult mentor whom I trusted, my teacher, took it from me.

It is also my hope that the process of writing this memoir may allow me to regain respect for a venerable organization, the Sisters of Charity of Cincinnati, which failed me again in 2003 when I went to them, forty two years after the abuse began.

Since then, my pleas for assistance have been repeatedly ignored. In "covering up" for the Sister Rita Celine, the President and Executive Council of the Sisters of Charity of Cincinnati have failed the adult me, just as Sister Rita Celine failed me as an idealistic adolescent. Ultimately, with or without their support, I must act upon sustaining an ancient wisdom, "To Thy Own Self be True," which is what I am compelled to be now.

I hope to forgive myself for allowing myself, as an adult, to once again believe in and be vulnerable with the Sisters of Charity of Cincinnati. After forty-two years, I left myself wide open to be traumatized once again, only this time, by the President, the Executive Council, and some members of the Sisters of Charity of Cincinnati from September 2, 2003 to the present time. I should have known better!

In addition, I write this painful story to put it into the public arena where it may create broader discussion of the Roman Catholic Church's deeply closeted and secretive practice of protecting those who commit child and adolescent abuses. The institution has fought resolving this matter with priests and has never meaningfully addressed, perhaps, the less blatant issues of predatory Religious Women. Countless numbers have been deceived and damaged by misfit Priests and Sisters whose crimes and sins are only magnified by the Church's subsequent silencing.

Only in the last years has the Roman Catholic Church given lip service of "We are sorry," while continuing to cover up pedophile priests and their supervisors. They put out money only when legally they were caught in lies and cover-ups.

I believe it was in 2018, when Pope Francis said he would have "ZERO TOLERANCE" for pedophile priests. I believe him in spirit, however, I don't know in practice what Pope Francis' actions might be.

A pedophile priest, as a pedophile religious woman, should be striped of their title, handed over to law enforcement, and imprisoned when found guilty. What these pedophiles have done is a sin and a crime.

Finally, in February 2019, Pope Francis had scheduled Bishops to come to the Vatican to discuss what to do about the sexual abuse by priests. The outcome? We are waiting!

Anyone who has been, or suspects someone has been, sexually abused by a religious person can help that person feel he or she is not alone in this distress. My memoir is intended to help empower those victims who have been shackled by the shameful behavior of those we trusted—individuals and their enabling institution, the Roman Catholic Church.

To break the cycle of sin and cover-up crime, I am compelled to tell this life story. Too many innocent children and adolescents have been physically raped, emotionally controlled, and spiritually damaged and broken by the so-called "Brides of Christ."

Then, they have been manipulated, as I was, into the ugly secrecy of silence. My continued failure to speak out against sisters' sexual abuse would be a lie, a sin of omission which would leave me co-opted with the Roman Catholic Church, the Sisters of Charity of Cincinnati, and their denial of my sexual abuse.

But, I also write to give others hope. Although the sexual abuse changed who I was, I still had the God-given power to build a successful, rewarding life. Years of therapy helped me to learn who I am—a strong, caring lesbian woman, capable of earning a MSSW. I am now seventy-five years of age, retired after a successful career as clinical social worker, and a small business owner. We have within us an inner strength that allows to reconnect to our spirit.

I wish to acknowledge that the rotten apple Rita Celine has been, has not deterred me from experiencing religious women who have remained true to their vows, holy, spiritual and human. I personally know some Sisters of Charity of Cincinnati who have lived out their lives in causes for social justice, social action for humanity.

Lastly, I wish to educate those who have not experienced sexual abuse. Please understand why you should not blame the victims and survivors. Please be watchful and protective of our children and adolescents. Please keep an eye on secretive adults whose behavior may be suspect. Adult actions and behavior must match their verbalizations, and this must always ring true.

In closing, some might argue that a book about women abusing women shows us to be our own worst enemy. Yet the problem of evil is surely not gender restricted.

In Western culture what happened to me is a crime. In the religious culture, it is labeled a sin. Enforcing rules against such behavior is extraordinarily difficult. The abuse is not seen; what is seen is the victim's valiant efforts to pretend to be normal.

My case is surely representative of many—as an adolescent I was emotionally manipulated, then sexually abused, and ultimately spiritually wounded. Each aspect of this descent was characterized by distinctive female underpinnings, as my seduction and disempowerment proceeded.

She wove a silk web. Only the best for this "classy lady," as she was known in Dayton, Ohio. She attracted me like a Black Widow. The more I became entangled, the more the silk turned into fishing line, an invisible but sturdy web. Some days I felt consumed by this web. Some days this web was so tight that I could hardly breathe.

When I finally discovered the strength to speak out, the question was, whom could I tell? Who would believe an adolescent speaking out against a pillar of the Dayton community? Who would believe a mere girl, a former Postulant who was twice asked to leave the Sisters of Charity of Cincinnati congregation, the same institution where Sister Rita Celine was esteemed?

So I remained frozen and silent like a deer in the headlights. I dare not confess. But finally, I have found the strength to do so and ask you, reader, to reexperience my story. Then, please share it with those who might care.

"To all the girls who have faced injustice and been silenced. Together we will be heard."

—Malala Yousafzai

CHAPTER ONE

LOSS OF INNOCENCE

I was fifteen when I met Sister Rita Celine Weadick, Sister of Charity of Cincinnati at Saint Joseph Commercial High School in Dayton, Ohio, in 1959. The Sisters and upper-class students at St. Joe's were having an Open House to introduce the high school to prospective students.

The audience gathered in the school's auditorium where Sister Magdalan Delores Harrington, Sister of Charity, the Principal, and others were speaking into the microphone. At that time, I was probably a pretty average teenager—tall and thin, cute with straight brown hair and brown eyes, gregarious with a quirky sense of humor. I was in the back of the bright room with its immaculate, freshly polished wood floors and was interested in the message of the speakers.

One was slight-framed in her black garb, with brown eyes, a wide smile and a certain way of cocking her head to one side then the other. After the presentation, some of us went to the speakers' platform for conversation, and I remember how admiring girls surrounded Sister Rita Celine.

It was obvious that she was charismatic and popular. I, too, was drawn to her and tried to act nonchalant as I walked through the periphery of the crowd to get closer to this Sister. She seemed to be the youngest of the sisters, perhaps in her late thirties, and had dark eyebrows, highlighting her brown eyes, which gave her face inviting warmth. Sister Rita Celine looked my way appraisingly, noticed me and smiled. I felt special.

I was a product of the local Catholic school system and had completed my freshman year at the Sisters of Notre Dame de Namur's Julienne High School, which was known in Dayton as the college prep school.

Catholic boys attended Chaminade High School. The Notre Dame Sisters had taught my siblings and me during eight years of elementary school. I was already considering switching to the other Catholic girls' alternative in Dayton, Saint Joseph's Commercial High School, that emphasized general studies, shorthand, typing, and work ethics.

This training was designed to give students local employment options, which was attractive to my parents. Also, I had struggled with academics my whole life, but did not learn for many years that I suffer from dyslexia, which, unacknowledged, lowers self-esteem and makes academics extremely difficult.

This background brought me that morning to hear the recruiters from St. Joseph's. In addition, I knew students at this school whom I admired, like senior Karen Sammons, who later became Sister Marie Karen, Sister of Charity of Cincinnati, and others who had joined the recruitment program.

Sister Rita Celine was the star recruiter.

While I listened to Sister Magdalan Delores, I thought to myself, what a dynamic likable soul; later I knew her as the respectfully named "Maggie Dee." Petite, with a quiet manner, and great sense of humor, she was impeccably dressed in her pressed black habit, which only revealed an oval face with twinkling blue eyes.

Although I thought of her as an older woman, Sister Maggie Dee, was probably forty-five at the time, principal of St. Joseph's, and also Superior to the Sisters who lived in the Convent on Second Street. Many called her the "Spirit of St. Joe's," and that admiring reputation continued long after the High School was closed in an economy move, shortly after I graduated in 1962.

After that fateful open house, and with careful thought, I decided to transfer schools and entered the first sophomore class at St. Joseph's. Since seventh grade, I had believed that I might have a vocation for religious life, and realized that the Notre Dame de Namur Sisters were trying to recruit me. This order had European roots in France, whereas the Sisters of Charity of Cincinnati were a younger, American-founded order that I imagined would be less rigid.

It was well known that Sister Rita Celine was the person who got many young women "ready for Community" for the Sisters of Charity of Cincinnati. Karen Sammons told me Sister Rita Celine was preparing her for entrance after her graduation.

So, shortly after I transferred to St. Joseph's, I introduced myself and informed Sister Rita Celine that I was interested in discussing my potential for religious life. She mentioned remembering me from the open house and listened to my thoughts about having a Vocation, which is what it was technically called—a special calling from God to become "His Bride".

Sister Rita Celine explained her role in preparing and sponsoring many girls for the Convent; she offered to help me and said we should meet regularly. So, it began auspiciously—Sister Rita Celine meeting with me and talking about the future of my life as a Sister. I felt I was in good hands. I knew I was in good hands.

We began meeting in her classroom every other week. Signs reading 'GOD IS LOVE' were on all four walls. I believed Sister Rita Celine was generous to offer this time to me, especially since she would not be my homeroom and civics teacher for two more years. I was grateful for her guidance; flattered by her attention. I felt special, and I thought that I wanted to be just like Sister Rita Celine.

During Christmas of my sophomore year, our relationship began to change. It started after I delivered some of my mother's Christmas baked items to the Convent. (My mother was renowned in Dayton for her special holiday cookies and candy, and continued their preparation into her eighties.)

To deliver her package, I took the bus downtown to the Convent, which was across the street from St. Joseph's High School. I had arranged for an appointment, and the Sister who was in charge that day invited me in.

Several Sisters greeted me in the parlor, Sister Rita Celine among them. Though the other Sisters melted away, including, surprisingly, my sophomore teacher. Sister Rita Celine stayed. Somehow Sister Rita Celine and I were alone, sitting on the parlor couch. I cannot remember what we talked about, but that encounter, during the Christmas season, forever changed my life. From then on, Christmas time has always signaled challenge for me to retain a sense of control over my life.

The sadness of the holiday season for many years has found me wasting days and months yo-yoing between numbness, rage, and severe depression. I have spent too much time pondering over the beginning of this relationship and how for me, Christ's birth became entangled in Sister Rita Celine's overpowering presence and subsequent clouding of moral questions about fairness, mercy, and justice.

That Christmas, Sister Rita Celine became "Rita" to me, a person who hugged me and lightly brushed my right cheek with her lips. She thanked mother and the family for the gifts and extended her regards.

In those moments, I felt pleased because I had brought happiness to the Sisters. Rita was happy; my mother was happy; I was happy. I felt great. What irony that this wrongheaded and prideful event was really about sadness and loss, for the Christmas affection from Rita was the beginning of a seduction which I was not to understand for many years, despite studying psychology as a therapist, having clients who experienced sexual abuse, and working with my own therapists.

We began meeting in Sister Rita Celine's homeroom where she was never demonstrative, but, was in fact, rather distant. I dutifully cleaned blackboards, stapled papers, and listened to Rita talk about the religious life and being a teacher. Eventually, she explained that she did not like casual physical contact with people, and held back from hugging or kissing.

I realized that clearly I was an exception. I also saw her every day during the week because Monday through Friday, Sister Rita Celine would either come to the table where I was at lunch, or run into me in the gym where most students fast danced before afternoon classes.

When my junior year arrived, on Saturdays I took the bus to Mass at St. Joseph's Church. I proudly walked behind the Sisters as they moved in orderly fashion from the Convent to Church. Still in their black habits, I amused myself, at times, thinking how they looked like penguins, a huddled mass of black, walking in unison, akin to military precision. But, I was at the end of that line! After Mass, Rita and I would often meet, and sometimes Sister Maggie Dee gave her permission for us to visit in the Convent parlor.

Before long, Rita was meeting me in the church vestibule after the other Sisters were seated in the front pews. She sat with me in a pew behind the other Sisters and held my hand under her habit. Then I followed her to Communion.

The Sisters had breakfast after Communion, as was the Catholic Church's rule then, that no one was to eat after midnight before receiving Communion.

Since I had not eaten, at first I grabbed a bite at White Castle or Simple Simon Restaurant, but soon I packed a peanut-butter-and-jelly or honey sandwich. I needed to save my precious babysitting money, which was fifty cents an hour in those days, earned from my older sister Carol's overflow business. I had little "spending money" then, as my family did not believe in allowances, and my mother required me to bank a fourth of my income. So, after having eaten, sitting in the Convent parlor meant a brief chance to talk and usually ended with Rita's hug and goodbye kiss on my cheek.

I needed to earn more money than fifty cents an hour from babysitting to help pay for school tuition. In the winter of 1961 Sister Maggie Dee found me a job at a bakery, so I worked after school until six, and on Saturdays from eight to six. Therefore, our after school and Saturday visits were discontinued.

In my senior year, Rita and I saw more of each other since she was my homeroom and civics teacher. She also supervised the St. Joseph's school library, where my mother was a volunteer. They became friendly, maybe friends, which pleased me and added to my feeling special.

Presumably because of my schedule constraints, Rita became more clever about finding free time and ways for us to be together. She arranged for us to meet, not in the Convent's parlor, but in St. Joseph's Teachers' Lounge on Sunday afternoons.

The routine became my having family dinner at one, then meeting Rita at three. She gave me a key to the high school so that I could unlock it and go to the Teachers' Lounge before she arrived.

As I waited for Rita, I poked around the refrigerator where leftover food and beverages, even beer, were kept from parish fish fries and festivals. I often sipped on the beer which Rita knew, but she never said anything to stop me, which I felt was really "cool" of her.

Rita never drank in my presence, though she told me that she needed wine to help with her pain, whatever that was. I never asked because in my family you worked through an illness, went to bed from exhaustion, and lay on a heating pad.

In the Teacher's Lounge, I recall the room's chairs, end tables with lamps, and white vinyl couch. The first time we entered this unlit quiet space, Rita moved a magazine off the couch, said nothing, and then motioned with her hand for me to sit down next to her. She always framed these visits as "special time because you are going into the Convent."

Today, I wonder if anyone ever asked Sister Rita Celine why we were together so much. I imagine she might have justified it by saying she was preparing Linda for Convent life. No one ever asked me about our frequent visits.

As our Sunday visits stabilized, Rita now took off her habit's headgear and put it on the end table. I, of course, admired her beautiful brunette hair. The couch was no longer the place where we sat, rather, we would lie together on it. Rita told me to lie next to her; later she directs me to lie on top of her, while we kissed, which seemed to go on forever. Should I make any movement, Rita would tell me to inform her, "If I felt anything down there" because, if so, we would have to stop.

Also, I was not supposed to wrinkle her habit. Thus Rita and I hugged, kissed, and pressed against each other. If I did feel something "down there," I most certainly said nothing to her because I was enjoying this unfamiliar experience. Rita convinced me that our affection was not sexual, only prolonged kissing was, and in my youth and naïveté, I believed her.

In 1961-1962 I was, not only a virgin, but totally without any sexual education from my parents, school, or friends, and had no sexual experience. Being a good Catholic girl, I had never even masturbated and did not learn for several years how to insert a tampon.

As an average teenager in Midwest Ohio, I dated several guys, Catholic only, and our platonic relationships were presented within the safe framework that "Linda is a good girl".

That meant I was a virgin and pure, which I was. When two different guys wanted to get more serious, I told them I was preparing for the Convent, so we drank too much beer and had a heck of good time dancing, shooting pool, going to sports events, movies, and driving through the Parkmore Restaurant.

I do remember our "making out," which meant kissing in their cars while worrying about the duration of a kiss. I did not know the exact length of time that the Church used to determine whether a kiss was appropriately short, a venial sin, which did not have to be confessed; or was a dangerously prolonged kiss, a MORTAL SIN needing to be confessed to a priest while also asking for absolution.

There was little to fear because my dates usually had a plastic Jesus or Blessed Virgin Mary statue on their dashboards. I watched the statue out of my peripheral vision, praying to it while I was enjoying the kissing and simultaneously begging God for clarification about the appropriate duration for the kiss.

My high school years at St. Joseph's are something of an emotional mixed bag today. I recall that I went through a sorority initiation, with mostly students I knew from Julienne High School, and I was voted sorority treasurer.

I also remember realizing that the sorority was seen as exclusive and cliquish; my egalitarian nature kicked in, and I dropped out. I recall that in 1962, I was named Festival Queen.

My mother gave me a new dress for this honor: a beautiful form fitting long sleeve paisley dress, which fell just below the knees. This was a big deal because, up until then, I only had skirts and blouses, jumpers for dress up or my dark green school jumper uniform worn with a white, long sleeved blouse.

The happy memory of being voted Queen and the gift of my first grown-up dress from Mom is darkened by the altercation it sparked with Sister Rita Celine. She wanted me to sing, *Oh, my name is McNamara, I'm the leader of the band,* as I entered the auditorium with my attendants.

The prospect embarrassed me, and I declined. We were standing in the corner of the auditorium, which served also as the gym, and a class was practicing basketball. I felt uncomfortable having this disagreement in public. Sister Rita Celine stared with a black look in her eyes, head tilted up. She became quietly angry, walked away, and punished me with her silence and removal of visitation rights.

Finally, I agreed to sing on the condition that the other attendants would sing as well. After this episode, I made a mental note that crossing Sister Rita Celine could interfere with my Convent admission, so now I had to obey her, as well as my parents.

Sometimes, I was frustrated by the conflict of wanting time with my family and school friends, and Rita's demands. But most of the time, I was at this teacher's "beck and call," and thoughts of her consumed my waking moments. Clearly I was preoccupied, even mesmerized, thinking about our next visit.

At the time of graduation, each homeroom student received a graduation present from Sister Rita Celine—a small piece of pink paper rolled up and tied with a white ribbon that read as follows:

GOD IS LOVE. TO MY HOMEROOM OF 62—once again it is time to bid adieu to another dear group who are no longer students but friends.

As students I want to thank you for your daily friendliness and cooperation. As your homeroom teacher I say in all sincerity I have enjoyed each day I have been with you. It has been said that life is but a movement of love from the heart of God and back again to God's heart and in this flow of love we come to know and love others. I believe this is true and here is where I met you. He willed you to be my Class and in meeting you, knowing you, I have meet and known a new beauty of Christ for in each of you God has placed something of His own beauty in your human personality.

At this time when words of advice are common I would have you remember this saying, that there is only one failure in life NOT TO BE A SAINT for this reason God gave you life. You remember His wishes and He will remember yours.

Though life may not hold that we meet again here on earth yet I trust Christ will keep you and this is my prayer for you.

This June 14 shall be offered for your intentions Linda and also I promise you that you will remain always in my prayers until we meet for good in ETERNITY.

May God love and keep you,

Sister Rita Celine*

During graduation week I received a small black leather binder from Rita. In it she placed an unsigned partial copy of the above, which read:

Life is but a movement of love from the heart of God and back again to God's heart and in this flow of love we come to know and love others. I believe this is true and here is where I met you. He willed you to be my . . . (Rita did not continue.)

Thus, our mutual attraction was a manifestation of God's intention.

Before commencement, I had applied to the Sisters of Charity of Cincinnati to enter their Postulancy. To my surprise and hurt, I was denied acceptance because as Mother Mary Omer Downing, Mother General of the Sisters of Charity, informed Sisters Rita Celine and Maggie Dee, my mother had threatened to sue the diocese if they admitted me before I was of legal age, which was nineteen in 1963.

---

* I do not have a copy of this document as I gave it to Sister Pat in 2007 during my investigation review.

Everyone was shocked. I confronted my mother about this roadblock, saying that I had my own life to live. She was even more passionate. Startling me, she responded, "I would rather you told me you were pregnant than that you want to enter the Convent."

I was stunned. How could she be surprised about my plans, and how could anyone raised in the Catholic faith reject the idea of its being an honor for parents to have children enter religious life? For decades my family served the "people of the cloth". They tithed, paid school tuition, and volunteered for everything: washing, starching and ironing linens for the alter to be used at Mass, running church bingo games, fish fries, festivals, and serving on various committees and boards.

It was an impasse. I could not afford to leave home, as my two older siblings had done after graduation, and was stuck there, alone with mother's disapproval and Dad's silence.

The Convent's wheels were still turning and, though I had resigned from my job at the baker, Sister Maggie Dee promised to find me employment; this was, after all, one of her functions at St. Joseph's Commercial High School.

What she came up with was unique; I was to be called Assistant Secretary to the Secretary to Sister Magdalan Delores, be paid $100 per week, which was not to be declared as legal income.

Although my innocence extended to most financial matters, my mother had taught me the difference between gross and net pay when I took the bakery job, so I knew I would be making very good take-home money.

Hindsight suggests that this was a made-up job that kept me

under Sister Rita Celine's thumb. "Assistant to the Secretary" was invented briefly for me. I typed schedules, bulletins, and thank you notes to donors. My office at St. Joe's was between Sister Maggie Dee's office and the library. Having Sister Maggie Dee nearby was pleasant; she called me her "all American Girl."

However, I always had to be on guard for Sister Rita Celine's unexpected visits before or after her classes, or lunch, or after school. It concerned me that Rita would close the door and press me against a sink in my office.

She took the most amazing chances, and I knew enough now to realize that her behavior, and consequently, *our* behavior was questionable, even though Rita reassured me that *our behavior was physical, not sexual*. Her hold on me was firm.

Meanwhile, whenever I was enjoying life outside of St. Joe's, I had to remember that Sister Rita Celine had instructed me to call her at specific times, which I did, no matter what was happening. I told no one. I dared not challenge Sister Rita Celine who subtly reminded me that entering the Convent depended upon her sponsorship.

When I try to evaluate how she escaped censure, I still wonder how much the other Sisters knew or suspected. Sister Rita Celine was attractive and often aided Sister Maggie Dee who had to wine and dine local businessmen in Dayton to gain their financial support for the Commercial High School.

Since Sister Maggie Dee also sought employment for the graduating Catholic girls, who were well trained in business techniques, she served a valued role in the community. Today, I cannot bring myself to believe that the Superior of the St. Joseph Convent Sisters, Sister Magdalan Delores, knew how badly Sister

Rita Celine was behaving, though she favored Rita and trusted her obviously too much.

Then Rita upped the ante again, saying that we needed more quiet time together before I entered the Convent. I believed that she was preparing to give me the inside scoop on how to succeed in convent life.

I was to take her to a retreat. We were to share a twin bed, in a hot dorm room with no air conditioning. When we arrived, I went out for iced drinks and was surprised on my return to see Rita without her headgear or habit; both folded over the chair, as well as something that looked like a heavy, long rubber panel that might have been an undergarment.

I had never seen it before and did not touch any of this regalia, since I was taught that the habit was sacred. Seeing her out of her habit embarrassed me. I did not know where I was supposed to look, where to place my eyes, or if I was somehow not to notice. I wished, in a recent high school graduate kind of way, to be cool, so I feigned nonchalance, looking down at my reddish-brown penny loafers.

By then I knew the drill. First we sat, then lay down, then I was told to be on top, then pressing was okay.

Afterwards we ate and, finally, talked about my entrance into the Convent.

Her advice was: "Follow the rules, keep quiet," and then she stunned me by adding, "In a few years we can live together."

I felt as if she were promising a scene from the musical, *The Sound of Music,* except in this version we would each be climbing the mountain, meet at the summit, kiss (briefly), hold hands, and skip along while singing God's praises and doing good works.

Linda in First Grade in 1950.

Holy Communion Sacrament in 1951 or 1952.

Below: Immaculate Conception Grade School in 1951 or 1952. I'm here

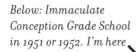

Rita Celine Weadick, SC

Born: October 10, 1922
Eaton, Ohio
Entered: September 7 1945
(51 years)
Died: December 27 1996
Good Samaritan Hospital

S. Rita Celine Weadick, 74, ministered 37 years in the field of education as a high school teacher and guidance counselor.

S. Rita Celine was raised in Eaton, Ohio. She grew up on a horse farm and loved horses as did her father After high school, Sister completed her bachelor's degree at the College of Mount St. Joseph. "Many college activities were curtailed because of the war but, in spite of this, my four years of college were happy ones," she said. S. Rita Celine entered the Sisters of Charity after graduation.

She began ministry in education as an intermediate teacher at St. William School (1947-50) in Cincinnati, Ohio, but spent most of her years on the secondary level. She taught at St. Joseph Commercial High School (1951-64) in Dayton, Ohio, and worked as a guidance counselor at Elizabeth Seton High School in South Holland, Illinois (1964-67). Continuing her counseling, Sister served in Kettering, Ohio, at Alter High School for ten years and as the librarian and counselor at St. Charles until 1984.

"It was S. Rita Celine's love of being a Sister of Charity that emanated from her," stated her longtime friend, S. Marie Karen Sammons. "People saw in her the love of God and they were naturally attracted to her. Many young people were influenced by S. Rita Celine." She helped many young women prepare to enter the Sisters of Charity

Her decision to leave education led Sister to a new ministry at Good Samaritan Hospital in Dayton as a technician (1986-89). Since her retirement in 1989, she continued to do volunteer work at Maria Joseph Home and Good Samaritan Hospital. S. Rita Celine was still volunteering at the time of her death. In all of her ministries, people spoke of Sister as a kind person and a "classy lady " Sister was buried December 30 in the Motherhouse cemetery

Obituary of Sister Rita Celine, SC, who died on December 27, 1996, written by Marie Karen Sammons, SC.

"You must do the thing you think you cannot do."

— Eleanor Roosevelt

CHAPTER TWO

FINALLY BEING ASCETIC

In the fall of 1963 at legal age 19, I entered the Sisters of Charity of Cincinnati. Before I left home, my mother and I argued; she accused me of "having a homosexual relationship with that woman."

I had to get a dictionary to look up the word "homosexual." While reading the definition I hung on every word, saying to myself, "No, no, no that's not what we do because Rita says what we do is physical, not sexual."

Entrance day arrived. Sisters Maggie Dee and Rita drove into our driveway. I tried to say a quick goodbye to my parents, but kissing my mother led her to say, "Is this the kiss of Judas?"

My heart raced as my feet flew to the car. I don't remember any conversation during the drive from Dayton to the Motherhouse in Cincinnati. What I do remember was the impression of the huge, black, wrought iron gates that protect the entrance of the avenue to the Sisters of Charity Motherhouse.

I do not even remember taking the required black trunk, but somehow it got to the Convent with me. I also remember being in the stunning chapel and the sweet, smiling eyes of Sister Emily

Anne Phelan, the Postulant Mistress.

Despite all of my preparation, being a Postulant was an ambivalent experience for me. Our daily schedule began with rising, washing, dressing, and being in my assigned pew within fifteen minutes for six o'clock Mass. After Mass the congregation quietly prayed for ten minutes before breakfast in the Refrectory with its long narrow tables dressed in white linen tablecloths.

Postulants were not to speak from sacred silence at nine PM the previous night until returning to the Postulancy after breakfast. The Postulancy consisted of a classroom with student desks and a study-library room across the hall, which had historical artifacts and photos of Sisters on various missions. The Postulant Mistress' office was located down the hall.

I was a freshman studying Liberal Arts general studies, carrying fifteen credit hours at the College of Mount St. Joseph on the Ohio, getting used to a foreign lifestyle, and experiencing a variety of emotions, including being angry, which I could not understand.

My "cell" consisted of a single bed, oak chest of drawers and chair, surrounded by a floor length white curtain like those found in hospital rooms. The white wall above my head held only a crucifix. The room had four "cells" which were silent as they were off limits to talking. The "cells" were only for sleeping.

I enjoyed starting lifelong friendships and some parts of religious living, especially meditation and solitude, which I continue to incorporate into my daily morning routine. Years later, I realized that one of the reason I was upset was that Sister Rita Celine would often encouragingly kneel or sit in the Motherhouse chapel with one of the Juniorates she sponsored for the Convent, but she was careful always to avoid my presence.

On the other hand, Sister Emily Anne was especially kind. The problem with the Postulant Mistress was that she was an "old school" sister, doing her best in attempting to incorporate recent, but not formalized, Vatican II relaxed directions.

I, and many of the other Postulants in the 1960's, wanted to pursue a more fashionable social justice and action philosophy. Could any order of traditional sisters incorporate changes in the tumultuous sixties? The Postulants were in a fishbowl at the Motherhouse, as members of the old establishment watched our every move. We became labeled "The Women of the Sixties," and that was because we questioned rules.

A few of us got together for discussions of the coming Novitiate, which was a probationary year of membership in the Congregation. We were interested in the vows of Poverty, Chastity, and Obedience.

Poverty was of particular interest to our social justice activism and was ethically motivated, as it was the one vow that connected us with the rest of the world. However, we lived with glaring violations in the Motherhouse—the exquisitely beautiful, expensive oil paintings, other impressive art such as huge vases and statues, elaborate parties, and both quantity and variety of daily food.

My peers chose me to address those present in the rectory about our concern of having two entries at every meal, and the quantity of food available when people were starving. These were illustrations of our lack of poverty.

I agreed to be spokesperson, but only if we were allowed to speak in the refectory. At evening meal, if we were permitted to speak, we each took a turn sharing happenings of our day, while perfecting cutting an orange peeling without breaking it, or was it correctly slicing a banana skin while eating the fruit with a fork?

Anyway, I remember nudging eyes beckoning me to speak. With frustration and exasperation, I timidly broached the subject. Paraphrasing, I said, "We are studying the Vow of Poverty, and we having two entrees tonight, as we've had at every meal since we've been here".

Now I was gaining steam, so added, "We should not have sacred silence at nine PM; we should be on the streets helping people." Then further adding, "We need to get rid of these 'Nunny' shoes and garbs because we stand out and get special treatment."

I sat down—exhausted. I remember silence, then cleaning a spot on the white linen tablecloth with a small brush and water and placing a bowl under the damp cloth.

Rules were a constant reminder that we had entered a strange land. Among other things, we were taught custody of the eyes, which meant we did not give direct eye contact to anyone, and looked down, unless we were engaged in a conversation, or being instructed on more rules.

We were also warned against particular friendships, which were never defined, but we were told only to be in a group. Years later, I learned this was to guard against lesbian relationships. Family visits were only allowed once a month, and my sister Carol came faithfully. She brought gifts, and even sent or brought food for the seventy other Postulants. I was quite alone since my mother had disowned me when I entered the Motherhouse, and thus never visited. Nor did my Dad, who kept the peace by placating his wife. It was stressful and lonely.

During one of Carol's visits, she said that Sister Rita Celine had sent her a letter with instructions to have me go to a room at the Motherhouse for a visit. This confused me, yet I was excited to be visiting with Sister Rita Celine.

I remember the room had a piano and no lights on. I thought, when people visit they don't sit in a dark room. I saw Sister Rita Celine in the corner, smiling and waving for me to come to her. I was so happy to see her, but she quickly grabbed me pressing herself upon me.

I was stunned that this happened in the Motherhouse and in a fog. I went to chapel, and crazily thought, "I can't remember saying goodbye to Carol." After this incident, I saw Sister Rita Celine also in chapel, kneeling with a Junior. In the future, Rita and I never spoke of this crazy-making event.

Better memories are of the Mother General, Mother Mary Omer, whose office was usually considered to be off limits to Postulants. I remember first entering her office from a hallway; I was hanging out with the excuse that I was on my way to chapel. Suddenly a Sister came out of nowhere, asking me what I was doing or what I wanted. She was cuttingly direct, but not mean. I admitted that I wanted to see Mother Mary Omer, and she responded, "Do you have an appointment?"

I said, "No."

She said, "You have to have an appointment to see Mother," but did not offer me one. Suddenly, Mother Mary Omer appeared in the doorway, told the Sister it was all right, and invited me into the office.

Mother Mary Omer's office was as pleasant and sunny as she was. It was tastefully decorated in pastels and had a quiet air of kindness and respectability about it. Mother and I chitchatted for a while, and she said I could come back anytime. I took this literally and would "show up," but only occasionally, because I knew I should not make a nuisance of myself.

The Sister, who was Mother's secretary, put up with me, when I "popped in," asking if Mother had a few minutes. Finally, the secretary stopped asking me if I had an appointment.

These few visits were wonderful and, of course, helped me to feel good about myself. But more than that, Mother Mary Omer took time to draw me out, especially about my mysterious anger.

I will always treasure Mother teaching me that. "Anger is like a river meandering. Sometimes, however, it overflows onto the riverbanks, and this is not good."

She asked me what this meant, but I could not answer. This was the first time I had heard the word "meander," so I rushed to the library to look it up. But, when I first did not understand, Mother Mary Omer did not embarrass me, for she probably realized that I did not know what "meander" meant.

Then when she asked me the questions again, I could reply, "Because it would flood the land." And Mother smiled, and said, "Yes, and that is not good."

In my mind's eye, even today I can see Mother Mary Omer and her Council sitting in the back of chapel in their magnificent, large, carved wooden pews. Whenever I saw Mother sitting there, I would subtly wave, thinking no one saw me; she didn't wave back, though a few times when our eyes met, she winked.

At the end of the cold winter semester, I was called into the office of Postulant Mistress', Sister Emily Anne, This office was long and narrow, with a large dark oak desk and chair with two smaller chairs across from her desk, a wooden bookcase and a window.

The heavy wood furniture and her position created a serious, somber mood.

Sister Emily Anne informed me that I was not doing well in my college classes and offered two suggestions. One was I could decrease coursework, and the other was that I might become a domestic sister. I eagerly agreed to both ideas, adding that I always enjoyed cooking, cleaning, and manual work.

But, in my naiveté I did not realize that becoming a 'domestic sister' was considered to be a lesser role by some Sisters in the Community. Now, I wonder if the Sister was testing my humility, or trying to break my spirit. Could it have been a push to make me wish to leave the Convent?

I remained there through my freshman year. Then one night Sister Emily Anne came to my cell, parting its white, surrounding sheeting. She stood over me while I lay in bed appearing larger than her tall frame. Her words were quiet, or maybe they were falling on deaf ears. It was Sacred Silence so I knew what she was saying was serious, or she would not break the rule.

Sister informed that my sister Carol was picking me up in the morning. Shocked and stunned, I thought she was going to tell me my Dad had died. Mom had sent me a note around Thanksgiving time telling me I caused Dad to have a heart attack because of all the trouble I was causing entering the Convent.

Because it was Sacred Silence, I could not respond. That sleepless night I recalled the time when I spoke out in the Refectory and Rita's visit, and wondered one or both of these events caused me to be forced to give up my dream of becoming a Sister.

In the morning Sister Emily Anne walked me down the long, gray hall to the back of the building, where Carol was waiting for me in the parking lot. Despite the Motherhouse rule against having physical contact, or even saying goodbye, Sister Emily Anne hugged me, and I thought my heart would break. What would my Postulant friends, or pew partner, think when I wasn't there for morning chapel?

Years later, I encountered a few of those friends who told me how the Sisters handled such an expulsion. In one's words, "We were on a picnic, and after we ate and had a long walk, Emily Anne told us you left, and then said, "Eat your ice cream before it melts."

That was Convent life in the 1960's. It resembled the narrative in Audrey Hepburn's movie, *The Nun's Story*, when she was shunned because of the decision to leave. My sister, Carol, later gave me a copy of this movie, which I still treasure.

The entrance to the Motherhouse of the Sisters of Charity of Cincinnati in Mt. St. Joseph, Ohio.

Postulate
Mt. St. Joseph, Ohio

Dear Parents and Friends of our Postulants:

Greetings from the Mount and welcome to our large circle of friends. This letter comes as an explanation in regard to Postulant Visiting Sunday regulations.

The first regulation is ---- NO FOOD MAY BE BROUGHT TO POSTULANTS ON VISITING SUNDAY. This rule has come about because of the tremendous quantity of food received in past years, which caused us great anxiety in regard to its immediate use and waste. Much of it consisted of bakery goods, fruit and candy which could not be stored away for future use. We suggest a cash donation to a recreation fund which we use throughout the month. (This is merely a suggestion -- no obligation.)

The second regulation is -- ONLY THE FAMILY AND CLOSE RELATIVES MAY VISIT POSTULANTS ON VISITING SUNDAY OF OCTOBER, NOVEMBER, DECEMBER, FEBRUARY, APRIL AND JULY. OTHER FRIENDS of the Postulants may join the family on the VISITING SUNDAY OF JANUARY AND MAY. Because of Lent and Retreats, there are NO VISITING SUNDAYS IN MARCH AND JUNE. We hope this arrangement will prove more satisfactory to the FAMILY, than the former rule of <u>anyone</u> on <u>any</u> Visiting Sunday.

POSTULANT VISITING DAYS ----- 1963-64

1. Saturday, October 12, or Sunday, October 13, 1963
2. Saturday, November 9, or Sunday, November 10, 1963
3. Saturday, December 7, or Sunday, December 8, 1963
4. Saturday, January 11, or Sunday, January 12, 1964
5. Saturday, February 8, or Sunday, February 9, 1964
6. Saturday, April 11, or Sunday, April 12, 1964
7. Saturday, May 9, or Sunday, May 10, 1964
8. Saturday, July 11, or Sunday July 12, 1964

The time for Visiting is any THREE HOURS between 1:00 and 5:00 P.M.. Those who come only 3 or 4 times during the year may have all 4 hours. Those who come only once a year may visit on both days.

Please come to the main entrance of the Convent and a room for visiting will be assigned to you.

We know we can count on your cooperation. We depend on your good prayers and beg God daily to bless each one of you.

Thank you,

SISTERS OF CHARITY

Dear Mom and Dad,

Sister Emily Anne thought that this would be helpful I would surely be glad to see you on visiting day Remember that I always love you Lovingly,

This letter from the Postulant's Office of the Sisters of Charity of Cincinnati to my family announcing the visiting days for 1963-64, with my handwritten note to Mom and Dad at the bottom. Although my sister, Carol, came every visiting day and also brought food (against the rules), my mother and father never came to visit.

*My photo from when I graduated from
St. Joseph Commercial High School
in 1962.*

*My sister, Carol, was always there for me. Left: her graduation photo from
1954. Right: Carol at a special occasion in 1974. She died of diabetes in August
2000.*

Statue of Jesus at the Motherhouse.

View of the Motherhouse of the Sisters of Charity of Concinnati at Mt. St. Joseph, Ohio. The first building in the complex opened in 1886. It overlooks the Ohio River west of Cincinnati.

"Life shrinks or expands in proportion to one's courage".

— Anaïs Nin

CHAPTER THREE

A PRODIGAL RETURNS TO DAYTON

Carol had chosen to attend Dayton's public high school, which led to a job at Wright-Patterson Air Force Base. She now shared her one-bedroom apartment with me, where I slept on a living room hide a bed. My mother had disowned me for entering the Convent, stating that she would not return to Mass until I left the Convent and moved back home.

I never saw or heard from either Mother or Dad. First, I found a job at a blueprint company and then later, a car dealership in downtown Dayton. At that time, I took the bus, and still went to morning Mass at St. Joseph's Church.

Sister Rita Celine had been moved to South Holland, Illinois with Sister Maggie Dee, who was appointed Principal of Elizabeth Seton High School, a new venture for the Sisters of Charity of Cincinnati.

I could not afford a car, so I borrowed my sister's light green Chevrolet Corvair and went up on two weekends to visit them. I had little money for gas, and the trip from Dayton to South Holland was long. I worked weekdays, as did Carol, who usually needed her car on weekends.

Each time I made the trip it was the same. Some of the Sisters, including Maggie Dee and Rita, would greet me and say goodbye. Rita and I usually ate together in the guest dining area; sometimes Sister Maggie Dee would join us. We would go together to morning Mass, and sometimes evening prayers.

Rita said "Good night" with other Sisters around. As I look back now, I am conscious that she never hugged or kissed me in front of other people.

I am not positive whether Sister Maggie Dee was the Superior of the Sisters at that time, but I assume she was because Rita began to take extreme liberties with me. Wearing only a nightgown and robe, she would come to my bedroom in the guest wing around eleven PM and stay for an hour.

I would be in bed; Rita would climb in and, after an hour, tell me she'd be back in the morning around four-thirty. As promised, she would return dressed in her habit, remove her headgear, and climb back in bed, always reminding me not to wrinkle her habit. Then I would dress, and we would go together or separately to the Convent's chapel for morning services.

Between the autumns of 1964 and 1965, Rita surprised me by saying that her family's property was going to be sold in the future to make an airstrip. When that happened, she said, there would be money for us to enjoy. I couldn't absorb the meaning of "us", but was quite shaken by her excitement about inheriting wealth. I knew sisters took the Vow of Poverty, did not own anything, or have money of their own. So, I was surprised and puzzled.

Moreover, I could not think what money either of us would ever need to enjoy ourselves. In my family, money wasn't enjoyed; it mostly paid for necessities and maybe an occasional movie. What one was supposed to enjoy in life was free.

Several months after I left the Convent, I contacted Mother Mary Omer, seeking her counsel for possible reentry. We met in November of 1964, and she advised me to continue on my inner path, and to seek a spiritual director.

She suggested that I also remain in contact, live the Vows I hoped to take one day, and have fun. I still assumed that I would return to the Congregation, but in the back of my mind, I was also questioning Rita's behavior. I now knew that her coming to my bedroom without her habit and breaking Sacred Silence was against Church and her Congregation's rules, and was sinful. Since I had lived in the Motherhouse, I also better understood the Church and Congregation's meaning of Poverty, Chastity, and Obedience.

In the summer of 1964 or 1965, Rita asked me to drive her and another Sister to Michigan where she was taking a school counseling course at a university. I borrowed a friend's car and drove them to Michigan, but was upset. I was beginning to see the gap between Convent rules for monastic life and Sister Rita Celine's not living her Vow of Poverty. I challenged her about this, but she defended herself by saying that the Sisters of Charity interpreted these rules to cover "poverty of spirit."

I responded that was absurd, a justification for her behavior of overindulgence, and I would never help to finance her expensive tastes. Sure enough, in Michigan, Rita led me to her dorm room where, despite the heat, she locked the door, removed her headgear, then her habit, leaving on her slip and underwear. Suddenly, I broke out of my passivity, expressed my resentment, yelled at her, shoved furniture around and cried. Then I left Sister Rita Celine behind and drove back to Dayton by myself. She obviously found another way home from her summer course work.

After that incident, I withdrew from frequent contact with Rita and the other Sisters in South Holland. My sister Carol became my main source of comfort. She accepted my desire to reenter the Convent, so each of us thought that our time together was limited. We lived in her apartment together peacefully, with me cleaning the house and tidying up after dinner, while Carol did the grocery shopping and cooking. Friends came over to play board games and cards, and I even subbed on Carol's bowling league.

Following up on Mother Mary Omer's request I arranged for an introduction to Father Harold Diller, Society of Mary. He agreed to become my Spiritual Director, and we met for two years at his Rectory in Oakwood, Ohio; at first every two weeks, then once a month. Father Diller stayed in contact with Mother Mary Omer and assured her of my sincerity. His analysis of my problems at the Cincinnati Motherhouse was that I was "ahead of my time."

In 1966, Mother Mary Omer informed me that I had been recommended and accepted into the Postulancy, but would enter its branch in Pueblo, Colorado. It had been established for women in the West, so they could be close to their families until their Novitiate at the Motherhouse. I wondered why no consideration was made for my having to leave my comfort zone. I thought the Western Postulancy may have been prescribed to separate me from friends at the Cincinnati Motherhouse; remove me from a scene of previous failure, or it just might have had something to do with Sister Rita Celine.

My ever-loyal sister, Carol, helped with my plane reservations. Sister Rita Celine's advice amounted to a mantra about obedience to Convent rules. She also emphasized her post-Novitiate reward—our living together in the Community, which I did not understand, or dare to question.

Huddy Heathcliff Mahlmeister. Ageless.

I thank my parents for giving me a love of animals. My fur children have been a Godsend, and all have been rescued from shelters.

Marie Susie, age 10, on the pool deck.

Lucy, age 12. 2000.

Maggie May, age 12. 2016.

"ABOVE ALL, BE THE HEROINE OF YOUR OWN LIFE, NOT THE VICTIM".

— NORA EPHRON

CHAPTER FOUR

A POSTULATE AGAIN

When I reentered in the fall of 1966, there were only twelve of us in the Western Postulancy, all wonderful young women, sincere in wanting to live out their lives with God. I have nothing but fond memories of this group, and still have one dear friend, Jeanne, whom I met there. Again, my sister Carol came through with gifts, often homemade food for four to six professed Religious and twelve Postulants.

The Western Postulant Mistress was Sister Angelica Berghoff. It was as if she disliked me on sight, or in retrospect, perhaps before sight. We instantly clashed, and my life worsened during the six months I lasted under her rule.

Angelica represents for me women's inhumanity to women. Where this came from, what demons she struggled with, I have never been able to guess. An example from early in my stay there: I witnessed Sister Angelica verbally abuse two elderly Professed Religious; they stood in front of her like whipped pups while Sister Angelica berated, insulted, and screamed in their faces about a minor issue in the chapel.

My injured sense of justice took over, and I could not keep quiet.

In a mindless, knee-jerk reaction, I challenged Sister Angelica about this verbal abuse and told her to pick on someone her own size. I did not realize it then, but she took me at my word and subsequently used every possible occasion to humiliate me. The stage was set.

I received no mail from Sister Rita Celine while I was in the Western Postulancy, which was only a relief. From my point of view, I was giving my best personal effort to live the Religious Life and felt that I was making progress, despite Sister Angelica's constant criticisms. I believed I was getting better at figuring out which hat I was figuratively supposed to be wearing—one day a hat with "woman of humility" written on it, and another day one with "independent woman." I tried to anticipate which hat Sister Angelica wanted.

Then, and now, I truly believe this woman's passion was to break my spirit or drive me to quit, as she beat me into the gutter. Whether she had heard about Sister Rita Celine or my first Postulancy, I did not know, but her every test was designed for humiliation.

For instance, Sister Angelica put me in charge of the 'Community Closet' with strict instructions to inform her of anyone who asked for tampons. Community Closet is Convent talk for a designated area where all extra items are stored. For instance, you might come in with a tube of Colgate toothpaste, and after it ran out you could ask for a tube, but you might be given Crest.

Asking for supplies was supposed to increase humility; thus owning nothing was living out the vow of Poverty. After a month Sister Angelica called me into her office. She was seated behind her oversized power desk. When I sat down in the chair opposite her, I was literally backed up against the wall. I dreaded what was coming.

With jaw set, she asked me who had gotten tampons. I withheld the information. She jumped out of her chair, learned across the desk, almost spitting in my face, and said, "I know someone asked for tampons because some are missing." I was astonished that anyone would count tampons. I had never even used them, and certainly did not know if they brought pleasure, but figured Sister Angelica must think so, or why would she be so angry?

For me, on the other hand the larger issue was loyalty to the other Postulants, not "ratting" on someone. Consequently, I was relieved of Community Closet duty.

Sister Angelica then gave me another task, putting me in charge of the kitchen when our lay, black, female cook had time off. I was mainly to prepare breakfast on weekends and some holidays. At first, I got up about three AM and quietly sneaked into the kitchen in order to take the butter out to soften.

Then after Mass, I only had about ten minutes to prepare breakfast for eighteen, plus occasional guests. When I learned to trust the butter to soften, I let myself sleep in until about four-thirty. I would sneak into the kitchen to check things out, and then go back to my room to wait until it was time to dress for seven o'clock Mass.

Since we even had a specific time prescribed to dress, if I were caught walking to kitchen duties in pajamas and robe, terrible repercussions would follow. My plan was to plead a sleepwalking disorder.

I was handling the kitchen just fine, but Sister Angelica said she thought I needed help. So, she assigned another Postulant to kitchen detail. When I asked what duties each of us was to have, Sister Angelica smirked and said, "Oh, you will figure it out."

Of course, the young Postulant was brilliant in science and math, but had zero common sense. After bumbling attempts to negotiate our chores, I informed her that I would take responsibility for the food groups, while she should take care of the coffee, tea, and ice water.

Soon, one dark weekend morning, a whistle kept blowing, and my assistant was atwitter. Despite the requirement of Sacred Silence until after breakfast, I had to tell her the teakettle was whistling and to remove it from the stove's burner. This was news to her. To this day I am convinced that Sister Angelica placed this youngster with me to create frustration.

Another incident took place one morning, again at breakfast, which we served buffet style. I could hear Sister Angelica's footsteps louder than the others because she was always first in line, unless we had guests. I had just finished buttering the toast. I placed it in a white paper lined basket, turned around, and put it on the counter.

Sister Angelica was right across the Formica counter from me.

She picked up the basket and hurled it against the kitchen wall, toast flying everywhere. She glared at me and stomped out of the kitchen. I was in shock. We were all in shock. No one said a word. I don't remember cleaning up her mess, but I am sure I did, with the assistance of my sidekick Postulant who seemed to be quaking in her "Nunny" shoes.

That afternoon Sister Angelica called an unscheduled meeting for the Postulants and spoke about the danger of anger, of losing one's temper. We all thought that any minute she was going to apologize for her inexplicable outburst of rage that morning. I waited and waited. She failed to apologize. I never figured out why she hated me or what caused her anger, which made this Postulancy one of the most bizarre experiences of my life.

Shortly after this incident, Jeanne, another Postulant and friend, and I were sent out on mission from Pueblo to St. Joseph Convent in Trinidad, Colorado during Christmas season, 1966 and the beginning of January 1967.

Being away was a breath of fresh air. Jeanne was happy to be with elementary school children, which I observed as she talked and played with them. After she left the Convent, Jeanne became an elementary teacher and had a wonderful career. I, however, did not know what to do with these kids, nor was I interested in teaching.

I thought I had safely gotten through another threatening Christmas season. But I may still have been a bit out of control.

One evening at the end of Epiphany, Jeanne and I were put in charge of the night's entertainment. Of course, everything went through the Superior of the Convent. Our plan was to play charades and most of the Sisters participated. We were all laughing and considered the evening a success.

Our next task was to take down the Christmas tree. While were were removing the lights and ornaments, I suggested to Jeanne, "Instead of us dragging this dry tree down the stairs and out into the foyer, we could just open the window, and push the tree out. It would save lots of work and time. Otherwise, we'll have a big mess of needles to pick up in the stairways."

Jeanne agreed and went down to be sure the coast was clear, no Sister's lurking about. She came back upstairs and helped me get the tree through the open window. I held the tree while Jeanne went downstairs to recheck that no pedestrians could get hurt. When she gave the okay sign, I pushed the tree out of the window.

Mission accomplished, except that I stabbed my left hand on a nail at the bottom of the tree.

The wound bled profusely, as Jeanne helped me into the bathroom and wrapped my hand. We agreed not to say anything to the Superior because it might get back to Sister Angelica. Jeanne knew I was on thin ice with her, and Jeanne also did not favor Sister Angelica.

That evening, we sneaked around, and very quietly Jeanne washed and rolled up my hair. Fear was in the air; if anyone caught us, we might be accused of "particular friendship." At Mass the next morning, we could hardly keep from laughing. We sat in the same pew, and Jeanne had to read prayers. Needless to say, it was a tough morning.

I was ambivalent about my experience in the West. Some Sisters seemed to enjoy life, while others appeared quiet and even suspicious. Two special Sisters, whom I met and admired at this Convent, were Sisters Jean Therese Durbin and Janet Marie Wehmhoff. Both woman were lively, likable, and had a good sense of humor.

I thought the experiences I wrote to Carol about during this Trinidad mission were positive, but I included a comment that if I could get through the year with Sister Angelica, I would be home free. I had no reason to know or suspect that the Superior read Postulants' letters—all incoming and outgoing mail.

The letter to Carol must have been censored by the Trinidad Superior, then sent to Sister Angelica, and finally forwarded to Carol. This was something I learned only after my sister's death when I went through her important papers and found my letter to her postmarked "Pueblo" instead of "Trinidad".

When we return to Pueblo from mission, Sister Angelica was nowhere to be found. Rumors spread among the Postulants that she might be ill, and another Sister was temporarily put in charge.

Some time after this change, Mother Mary Omer arrived from Ohio for a western visit. The Postulancy was "spit and polish," bustling with excitement. I was delighted, felt special when Mother asked to see me, and thought we would have a wonderful visit.

I remember the visiting room being softly lit, decorated with comfortable blues matching Mother's eyes. But this day she had tears in her beautiful blue eyes and told me, "I have done everything I could, but Sister Angelica is convinced you do not have a vocation."

I was speechless, thinking how could she, the Mother General of the Sisters of Charity of Cincinnati, believe a bitch like Sister Angelica? Today, I continue to have great respect and love for Mother Mary Omer who died after the turn of the century. She was always kind, understanding, and provided mentoring.

Knowing her is why I decided to become a social worker, her desired profession. (She was not a social worker then, because the Community only had nursing or teaching.) My experience with Mother Mary Omer was that of faith-filled, saintly woman, a true exemplar.

A few days later, the Sister in Charge called me into her office, informing me that my sister Carol had made arrangements again for me to live with her. I do not know who this Sister was, and I would have liked to have had the opportunity to thank her. She took care of a parking ticket I received while driving the Community car in downtown Pueblo, where we had to go for "going away clothes," to wear on the flight back to Dayton, Ohio.

Jean Therese, SC (left) with students in Trinidad, CO in 1968 or 1969.

Jean Therese, SC with me and my Chevrolet Impala in 1967 or 1968.

Jean Therese, SC and Lucy in 2002. Lucy was named after Jean Therese whose biological name was Lucille.

Sins of our Sisters

2-13-2000

Dear Linda,
Cause that's
where all
good wishes
start!

❀

Happy Valentine's Day

No doubt about it —
this is already late!
Hope you *know* what a
special, dear Valentine
you *are*! My wish for

you is that you have
had some "renewal"
time since I saw you—
seems you are always
giving, do you really
take time to receive?
Just quietly take in
and revel in being loved?
One of my favorite little
books is *Let Yourself Be
Loved* — but that takes a
quiet heart *and* spirit —
I believe.
  Whether you want to
be or not — you are my
Valentine — and I thank
God for you. Much love,
  S. Jean Therese

One of the many notes Jean Therese, SC, sent me.

57

Postulant Friend

Linda —
   You are a people-maker
Look !
   You smile
   and they come to life
   You frown
   — they wilt
You pull within yourself — they
                         retreat
   But — when you aim belief at them
         they rush forth
      from all kinds of dungeons
      and they are beautiful !
      You are a people-maker !
               I love you, buddy !
                     Jeanne
                     12/68

A writing from my Postulant friend, Jeanne, after we were on mission in Trinidad, CO.

"I'M TOUGH, I'M AMBITIOUS AND I KNOW EXACTLY WHAT I WANT,
AND IF THAT MAKES ME A BITCH, OKAY."

— MADONNA

CHAPTER FIVE

THE PRODIGAL RETURNS AGAIN

I returned to Carol's apartment temporarily and recontacted the Marianists. Father Holley helped me to join a Peace Corps-like group known as Front Line. I moved into its Annex, the second floor of a bachelor's home on the west side of Dayton, and lived with three other female Front Liners.

Soon I was labeled Director of their daycare center. It was a paper title only since an African-American named Roberta actually ran the daycare. She was around 45, and I was about 25 years old. I was to be the official white face that met people who financially supported the Dakota Street Center, of which we were a part. I was told a white face received a better reception at that time in Dayton, Ohio.

All the Front Liners were paid seventy dollars per month, free housing, access to the neighborhood food pantry, and use of the VW van. There were eight of us at the Dakota Street Center. Because my function as Day Care Director began early in the mornings, I had dibs on the van. The problem was I did not know how to drive a stick shift. My friend John tried to teach me, to no avail. So, I decided to buy a car.

I had no money after leaving the Convent but I figured that was a minor detail. I was determined to buy a car. I discussed this with Sally, a friend from pre-Convent days. She knew a coworker who had a car to sell.

Now, I only needed money. Sally taught me how to get a bank loan. I really do not remember how I got a $35 a month loan when I only had $70 a month income—but I got it. (My mother would have had a fit had she known I got a bank loan. My parents rarely asked for credit, and when they did, it was always "ninety days, same as cash").

I still cherish that beautiful steel blue Chevy Impala with matching leather seats. Now, I only had to get an Ohio Driver's license.

Roberta took me under her wing, educating me about the children and their lives. She taught me about the neighborhood, and the rule for me not to step foot where my white face was not safe. Roberta graced me with her friendship, inviting me to her home for delicious meals except for one item—chitlins. She explained what they were—I ate one! Then, after I left Dakota Street, I eventually gave her my Impala convertible. I had a love for her.

While at Front Line, I met many fine people, especially my dear friend Carmen Rosa Cortez, who helped to shape my life. Carmen was a St. Joseph Sister for seventeen years.

She left the Convent for two reasons. First, she received a lot of prejudice from fellow Sisters because she was Puerto Rican, and her ministry was in New York City, where many Puerto Ricans reside. According to Carmen, some of her Sisters felt "these people were lazy."

So, when Carmen became ill with rheumatic fever, some Sisters pushed her to work, and the Superior of the Convent held back on her medical treatment. She must not refuse to do her fair share of the work.

Carmen's second reason for leaving the Convent was that she realized she had romantic feelings toward a priest. She did not act upon them, but felt living a Vow of Chastity was no longer reasonable. She made arrangements to come to Front Line before leaving the Convent.

Carmen was assigned to St. Joseph Orphanage in Dayton, and we became roommates after each of us decided to leave Front Line. She received a scholarship to the University of Dayton where she completed her Master's of Special Education degree. With Carmen's help, I got a job at Dayton's Catholic Social Services while I studied to complete my Bachelor's degree in Social Work. Her boss at the orphanage, Father Garland, was also director of Catholic Social Services in the area.

While attending the University of Dayton, Carmen fell in love with a philosophy professor. She would talk, talk, and talk about his wonderment! One evening, I said, "So, invite him to dinner." She did, and he accepted the invitation.

When Bob arrived, Carmen went outside to greet him. After awhile, I wondered what was taking them so long to come into the house. I went outside and saw that Bob was in a wheelchair. I had not previously been aware of that. I got the neighbor to help lift him up the four steps.

This is just one example of Carmen's unquestioned inclusiveness. Carmen only saw the glass half full, never half empty—she saw the donut, never the hole.

I introduced Carmen to my sister and they quickly became friends. She and Carol got Mom and me speaking with each other and, over time, we resolved our estrangement.

Carmen was a very spiritual person. I saw her as a female Don Quixote. She never met a stranger, only thought positively of people, and never had a mean thing to say about anyone.

I was her maid of honor at her marriage to Bob, and godmother to their adopted son. When Carmen's health worsened, the family moved to Fort Myers, Florida. She was principal of a special education school there when she died in 1993 from complications of rheumatic fever.

Her heart had been badly damaged from the inadequate medical care she received in New York while she was a Sister. Once again, I questioned the motives of the Sisters.

One of the fondest memories was joining her at her family's home in San Juan where I spent time with her friends and relatives. Carmen and I had a lasting friendship of mutual acceptance. As she said, in her Castilian Spanish accent, "We will always be sisters." Having her in my life during periods of disappointment, transition, and joy was a special gift. I am a better person for having known her.

Sister Rita Celine's life again intersected with mine when, around 1967, she returned to the Dayton area. Her assignment was to the Convent and school called Alter High School in nearby Kettering, Ohio. I deliberately did not call Rita and felt noting but numbness toward her. However, Sister Rita Celine called my sister Carol several times and told her to have me phone her.

This made me angry, and Carol knew it, but I still withheld the reason until 1981 when I confessed to Carol the history of Rita's sexual abuse. I finally called Rita in an attempt to get her to stop calling Carol and leave me alone. However, she had a request;

she needed me to drive her to Eaton, Ohio, on Sunday, and I reluctantly agreed.

In my beautiful Chevrolet Impala convertible, I proudly drove to Alter Convent to see Rita for the first time since I had left the Western Postulancy. I felt strange. We talked in the Convent parlor; she offered me gourmet Price's chocolate covered candy, which I can still see; the gold box had mostly milk chocolate with a few pieces covered in colored foil paper. I was taken aback by her apparent nonchalance.

She never asked me to explain the Western debacle or discussed my faith. What Sister Rita Celine did say cut me to the core: "Linda, you will never make it in college; you just are not college material".

I was shocked that she would say this to me because I felt my leaving the Convent had nothing to do with academics, and I was currently succeeding in university classes. Also, she was a teacher and counselor trained to be empathetic. This was mean spirited.

Something else was going on here, but before I could think it through, Rita shrewdly threw me a second curve ball. She said she needed my opinion. This was a new wrinkle, because she never asked my opinion.

The inquiry concerned my view of two people casually hugging or kissing as was now allowed by a policy that changed Convent Rules, post Pope John XXIII Vatican Council.

Rita objected to this change. What an irony, and what a head game. So I simply responded, "Do what you want to do. Hug and kiss only the people you want. It's your body."

Despite my coolness, I still let Rita lead me to the Teacher's Lounge at Alter High School, and history repeated itself. I was in a fog and hurting, but continued to obey and do whatever she demanded. I dreaded driving her the next day to Eaton, Ohio to visit her childhood home and relatives, but I agreed to do it. I gave Rita my word.

When I awoke in the morning, I was annoyed with her. During the drive I refused to visit her family. Their place was in a beautiful setting that reminded me of my father's childhood home. I dropped her off and agreed to pick her up later. Eaton Park, where I waited, was peaceful. I was not.

When I picked Rita up to drive back to Kettering, she instructed me to pull into a motel parking lot on West Third Street in Dayton, told me to get a room, and bring some dinner back. Like a zombie, I obeyed.

But when I entered the motel room, I saw Rita in bed with her clothes lying over a chair. I was enraged and told her to get up as we're leaving. Nonetheless, she placated me and said to join her in bed where she held me, but I do not remember anything else. I did not know then what I was experiencing, but in my clinical studies, I realized I disassociated. I do not remember the drive home that early evening.

Rita continued to pester me by calling me at Catholic Social Services where I worked. She did not have my new home phone number, and I asked Carol not to give it to her, but Rita never attempted to contact Carol again. I guess I made myself clear to Rita not to call Carol, or if she did, Carol never told me. I did not return her calls. Her manipulations continued, for instance, by involving a fellow Postulant I had known in 1963-1964.

Sister Julie Suba invited me to functions at Alter Convent, including an anniversary party celebrating Sister Rita Celine. I do not remember how many years she was celebrating in the

Congregation, but I declined. Julie later called me saying Rita was hurt and asked me to call her.

Perhaps I felt exposure, or just embarrassed, and told Julie I would call her. Rita insisted we meet, which we briefly did in 1968. I took her to an early dinner at the King Cole in downtown Dayton, an upscale establishment with beautiful French oil paintings and linen tablecloths topped with fresh flowers. I ordered chateaubriand. It arrived at our table on a teacart, covered with a silver dome and accompanying tray.

Surrounding the beef tenderloin were baby carrots, broccoli florets, asparagus, and petal shaped mashed potatoes. I wanted to show off and appear, outwardly, that I was functioning fine and very sophisticated.

Following dinner, we went to my apartment at Rita's request. She said she wanted privacy for what I thought would be our discussion. This was the first and last time Rita was on my turf. During this visit Rita coolly expressed "concern" that I might be "homosexual." This was only the second time in my life that I had heard that word, but I did not need to look it up this time.

I was then stunned by Sister Rita Celine's casual recounting that she had previously had relationships with two other girls and one of these young women, she said, turned out to be homosexual. I was staggered by her mean revelation, and struggled to grasp what was happening. I felt like I was in a whirlpool being sucked into darkness. First, she confessed a pattern of leading girls into sexual intimacy, and then she blames one of them for being a homosexual. What was she thinking?

I will never understand the workings of her unbalanced mind, or how she justified her long held policy that affection between us was *physical, not sexual.* How could Sister Rita Celine not see that she had adult responsibility in these relationships?

At the time I thought, how could she project her own aggressive behavior onto others? She was playing a devious head game with herself, and I was caught in the dangerous web of her denial.

By now, in 1968, while driving Rita back to the Convent, I finally knew our relationship had hit a dead end. I was ending it. Nonetheless, she continued to send letters and call me at work, leaving messages for me to call her. Rita invited me to a lake where Sister Marie Karen Sammon's family had a cabin, insisting that we needed to spend time by the water to "Talk over our differences." I did not respond to this letter.

Then she wrote that she was ill, and I must come. She is "crying wolf," I thought. It was more manipulation, and if she were really ill and asking for me, another Sister would call. Our shared contact, Julia Suba had died, so from that point on, I tore up any mail that came from Sister Rita Celine.

In the early 80's, during a therapy session, I said to my therapist, "Rita said what we were doing was physical not sexual'." My Jewish therapist said "Linda, there is no difference." I went into a blind rage, disassociated, and took down all of the pictures in her office. I found myself outside, sitting in my car. I realized I did not remember when our next appointment was, so I went back to her office.

My therapist was waiting at the door, and I followed her back to her office. I then saw the pictures on the floor and realized what I had done. Without any words spoken, I rehung the pictures and we scheduled several appointments beginning with the next day.

We role played several more times, and I felt I was ready to confront Rita. My therapist, Joan, agreed. She was willing to go with me and we role played the scene. When we came to the part where Rita Celine denied the sexual abuse, I said, "I would kill her." Joan said, "This is my concern for you because we know Rita will deny the abuse, being a Religious Woman, and I'd have to visit you in prison."

Joan retired and moved out of State in 1981, so around 1982 I was finally ready to confront Sister Rita Celine by myself. I was experiencing sleep disturbances and nightmares, inability to concentrate, and heightened feelings of anxiety and rage. With a few stiff drinks to give myself courage, I went to Alter Convent one weekend evening and asked for Sister Rita Celine. A small framed Sister answering the door told me that she now lived nearby with other Sisters.

I went into a Kettering neighborhood, drove up and over part of their small front lawn. Obviously, the Sister at the Convent called their house, giving them a heads up that I was on my way because when I went to ring the doorbell, a Sister immediately answered, letting me in without my asking for Sister Rita Celine. I was told to wait in the foyer. I remember I wore gray pleated slacks and a red long sleeved blouse thinking the color was appropriate for my anger. Rita came down a few steps, accompanied by two Sisters. I said, "I want to talk to you."

Sister Rita Celine responded, "I am not feeling well. Call me in the morning," then turned and went back upstairs. Those were to be her last words to me. I left, again another sleepless night "chewing" over all the things I needed to tell Rita in person, not over the phone or by letter.

But when I called the house about ten o'clock Sunday morning, well after morning Mass, I was told that Sister Rita Celine was unavailable; an hour latter I called again and got the same answer. This time the Sister introduced herself as Sister Marie Karen who added, "Sister Rita Celine is not available, and she will never be available to speak with you."

This intimidated me because Sister Marie Karen had told me years earlier that she had two brothers who were local police officers. Instead of challenging the Sister, I gathered together all of Sister Rita Celine's note cards to me, even the pictured holy cards with cryptic messages written on the back. One depicted a beautiful, modern-day Virgin Mary, holding baby Jesus that read: *In remembrance of our Christmas visit, and ALL that it held.*

Rita had organized these cards into a leather binder as a gift for me, including a professionally taken picture of herself, one in her old black habit I knew so well, and a second that she had mailed to me of her wearing the Convent's new, modified steel blue habit.

There were no pictures of the two of us, and I realized that we never had a picture taken together. Thinking about these mementos, I remember feeling the silken web turning into fishing line around my chest. I sobbed and tore up each note, holy card, and photo. I put them in a clay pot, which I took outside. I lit a match. I watched and cursed the flames because they did not do enough to consume my pain.

In 1986, I learned that Sister Rita Celine was volunteering at Good Samaritan Hospital in Dayton. I considered visiting her for a confrontation, but after discussing it with my next therapist, I did not.

Here is my fantasy: *The three of us, my therapist accompanying me, would sit at a table in the Hospital. I would tell Sister Rita Celine all the harm she had done to me, how its proper name is sexual abuse, and that her tricky "physical, not sexual" line was the ugliest lie of all.*

When Sister Rita Celine denied being a sexual abuser, I would take it as my cue to reach across the table, grab her by the throat and squeeze the life out of her. She is weakened, Code Blue is called, she goes to the Emergency Room and is revived. Rita cannot press charges because she dreads my public rendering of her behavior. Then Sister Rita Celine and I go to the Mother General and her Council where Rita confesses her abuse of several girls, including me.

Then the whole Community knows and each say to me, "I am so sorry for Sister Rita Celine's sexual abuse; I will pray for your intentions; here is a million dollars which cannot reimburse you for you victimization, but may offer some comfort. Sister Rita Celine will be confined in the Motherhouse, and we will move ahead in the Convent by training all of the Sisters about sexual abuse and providing college education for those Sisters who may be interested in working with victims and survivors." End of fantasy.

Without the relief of confrontation, I continued my search for peace. I joined a Bible study group and took classes on religion. I attended different churches; Catholic and others including Catholic Pentecostals, in-home Catholic Masses, Protestant Churches, and even Orthodox and Reform Jewish Temples.

When I attended Quaker services, I remember thinking that I need more than their "Light." The only surety I felt was that I wasn't an atheist.

During this period of searching, I sometimes longed for the simplistic life I knew as a child. Life seemed so clear then. Just follow the rules, and you were promised life ever after. You were not going to Hell. You would be with all the people you loved, your family and friends, your pets and wonderful neighbors. Just believe and tithe seven to ten percent of your earnings. Pay for special intentions (selling indulgences) and volunteer as needed.

With belief, all of this would get you to heaven, that wonderful life hereafter where you had no more pain, no more suffering, no more doubt. You were just at a wonderful banquet where all of your needs are met.

But now, as a mature woman, such a simplistic view of my spiritual journey felt hollow, a giant hoax perpetuated by a vast system of dogma and manipulation. I certainly did not conclude that all Roman Catholic people, Clergy, or Religious Women were evil, but I was questioning the hypocrisy and the dogma, which discouraged freethinking and exploration, and actually served to block my spiritual path. I was rage filled that I bought into the Roman Catholic Church and the Sisters of Charity of Cincinnati's propaganda time and again, leaving me disconnected from my true spirit.

On December 30, 1996, I learned that Sister Rita Celine Weadick died on December 27, 1996. A friend brought me her obituary from the *Dayton Daily News*.

Even in death, I felt her power over me. I cut out the obituary, putting her on a three-by-five file card and tucked it away. This comfortless end of my relationship with Rita elicited renewed nightmares and severe depression. I begged God for mercy and peace.

One of my nightmares is where I'm trying to escape Rita. I feel evil is present, Satan himself... I know that feeling well when He is present, and I experience the same occurrence.

It goes like this: I am in an airplane heading for the ground. The plane is shaking and the windows are cracking and I am trying to pull the plane up to prevent crashing. I am trapped. I am internally crying out, but nobody hears me because I do not have a voice. My soul is on fire, but nobody sees me, nobody sees my pain. The end.

Needless to say, I have difficulty flying!

Carmen Rosa Cortez—my female Don Quixote.

Left: Me and Carmen on the beach at Ft. Myers in 1984.

Above: At the Ohio River in 1969 while I'm showing her the Motherhouse of the Sisters of Charity of Cincinnati.

Left: Me and Carmen in 1968 going to a Christmas slumber party.

"It's supposed to be hard! If it wasn't hard, everyone would do it. The hard is what makes it great."

— A League of Their Own

CHAPTER SIX

EXORCISING DEMONS

On June 4, 1997, I woke up, sat up in bed, and said out loud, "John Christopher is the one." I believed God was telling me to talk with Sister John Christopher who was the Novice Mistress when I was a Postulant in Cincinnati. I knew that she was working at the College of Mount Saint Joseph on the Ohio.

That morning, still in extreme pain, I called the College. I asked to speak with Sister John Christopher. The woman answering the phone informed me that there was no one by that name listed at the college. I told her how I knew this sister, and she connected me to another person, a Sister of Charity who told me, "Sister Elizabeth Cashman used to be known as Sister John Christopher". She gave me Sister Elizabeth's telephone number in case we got disconnected, adding that she would try to connect me directly.

Sister Elizabeth answered the phone. "This is Sister Elizabeth Cashman, Assistant to the President. How may I help you?"

I froze. With great effort to speak, I managed to introduce myself and informed her that, "I was calling to put the Convent years behind me. I wondered if you would be available to meet with me."

My heart was in my throat and trying to escape through my head and ears. I had no saliva and shallow, labored breathing.

Sister Elizabeth said, "Yes," and my shoulders let down in relief. We set a time and date for me to come to her office at the college. I truly believed God was smiling with me, and I was accepting His free gift of "Yes!"

I drove to Cincinnati from my home in Centerville, Ohio following Sister Elizabeth's directions. I was a nervous wreck and reliving the first time I made the trip to the Motherhouse on Entrance Day. Then Sisters Rita Celine, Maggie Dee, and another Sister were in the car with me. I was nineteen.

During the drive, now in 1997, I was fifty-three, and I still felt scared as each mile passed. I began to cry and stopped myself as soon as a few tears dropped. I pulled out my "anger hat, and put on my clear Plexiglas "armor" to protect me. I chain smoked, popped peppermint Altoids, and rubbed my hands with vanilla lotion. As a middle aged professional woman, I obviously still felt intimidated.

When I arrived at the College, I changed parking places three times trying to get the closest parking spot so Sister Elizabeth would not have to walk so far. I did not know how old Sister Elizabeth was, but I figured she had to be elderly. I remembered that she had a deep voice as Novice Mistress, and at that time I must have associated the deep voice with old age.

I planned to be early, went to the first restroom I found, and freshened up. In planning the trip, I had also decided to go to Rita's grave, so I had placed a small pink impatiens plant and two lawn chairs in my trunk, in hopes that Sister Elizabeth would agree to go with me. I also took the crucifix Rita had given me from her Sister of Charity habit's beads. She gave me this gift when I reentered the Convent in 1966. She told me on a note card, "Think of me when you look at it, and soon we will be together."

"Think of me." That was the issue.

Arriving at the College of Mount St. Joseph on the Ohio on the morning of Friday, June 13, 1997, as scheduled, I went to the information desk and informed the young student working there that I had an appointment with Sister Elizabeth Cashman. She offered me a chair and called Sister Elizabeth's office.

A few minutes later a tall, slender woman walks down the stairs looking smart, wearing a chartreuse and black dress with black heels. I reminded myself that wearing the habit was rejected by the Sisters about twenty-five years ago in the mid seventies, following Vatican II. I recognized her smile, and she seemed to recognize me, or maybe she responded to me when I stood, as I was the only person in the waiting area.

We sincerely hugged, and I said I would like to go to Sister Rita Celine's grave. She offered to drive. I jokingly said, "Oh, you have your own car?" However, the joke was on me. She did have here own car provided by her Order, another change in their procedures.

I remember noting that she was not an old woman. I told her that I preferred to drive and laughed at myself for worrying about getting a parking space close to the door so she did not have far to walk. Sister Elizabeth Cashman knew exactly where Sister Rita Celine's grave was located in the Motherhouse cemetery, and seemed as sharp as I remembered her in 1963-1964.

I always wondered about that. I had not discussed going to Rita's grave. How did Sister Elizabeth know exactly where Rita's grave was? This was a huge cemetery. Perhaps, she suspected and was prepared for me. After we arrived at the gravesite, I took the two lawn chairs from my car's trunk, informing her that I wanted her to be a witness to my voice. Sister Elizabeth said nothing and sat down in her lawn chair.

Then I placed the crucifix on Sister Rita Celine's gray headstone, which said simply "Rita Celine Weadick, SC October 10, 1922 - December 27, 1996".

I began talking to Sister Rita Celine. I recounted the history of how we met, and that now I fully understood that her label for what she initiated between us, *physical, not sexual,* was, in fact, sexual abuse.

I interrupted my soliloquy to Rita, and, without looking back at Sister Elizabeth, I asked her if she was okay. She said that she was fine, and I proceeded with my narrative, ending with, "May God have mercy on your soul." The whole time Sister Elizabeth was as quiet as Rita's grave.

I planted the pink flowering impatiens, picked up the crucifix, returned the chairs to the trunk, and we left the graveyard. As we drove away, Sister Elizabeth asked if I could stay for lunch. At that time we were driving past the rear of the Motherhouse, when I forcefully commented I would never reenter the Motherhouse again. (This was the same parking lot that Sister Emily Anne, Postulant Mistress, ushered me to in 1964 when I left the Convent.)

Sister Elizabeth countered that we could eat at the College, adding, "I rarely eat at the Motherhouse myself." When we returned to the College, its cafeteria was closed, so Sister Elizabeth invited me to her office.

After I freshened up, we sat at a small round table just inside the door of her office. Sister Elizabeth looked at me with her dark brown eyes and said, "I believe you, and I am sorry."

Relieved and drained, I explained that I had needed her to be at my side to witness my voice, and that receiving her belief and sympathy was more than I hoped for. I explained that I had not wanted to come out with the truth while Rita was alive because I believed in her value as a pillar of the Dayton and Sisters of Charity communities. Moreover, I feared no one would believe me because I was twice asked to leave the Sisters of Charity Community, and now knew that I, myself, was a lesbian.

Without hesitation and emphatically, Sister Elizabeth surprised me by saying, "*Rita Celine was not a pillar to the Sisters of Charity Community.* We actually sent her away twice to alcohol rehab, I believe once in Michigan and another time to Massachusetts." Sister Elizabeth added, "At some Community gatherings, Rita Celine would be obviously inebriated."

My response was to explain, "I knew Rita drank wine, but to give the devil her due, she never drank in front of me."

It was time for me to leave, so I thanked Sister Elizabeth for her time, willingness to be a witness to my voice, and for believing me about Sister Rita Celine's sexual abuse. I said, "I hope I can now put the trauma of the Convent years behind me, but I know I can never put Rita's sexual abuse behind me. This abuse is my indelible scar and part of who I am."

Sister Elizabeth Cashman accepted my gratitude, and said she was glad to have been of help.

Before I left, I asked her if my old friends, Sisters Jean Therese and Maria, were still alive? Sister Elizabeth said they were respectively in Kettering and Dayton, Ohio and gave me their current phone numbers. After dropping out of their lives for over thirty years, I wished to reconnect. Before I drove away, Sister Elizabeth and I hugged goodbye, and I believed that I would never see this powerful woman again.

Driving home to Centerville, I was on cloud nine. In my mind's eye, I replayed and replayed the events and conversations of the day. I was so grateful to God that Sister Elizabeth had witnessed my voice, and believed me. I was peaceful, contented and so happy that I promised God, "I can now return to the Catholic Church, and will search out a Church community where I can connect and become an active dues paying member again."

I was relieved that someone from Sister Rita Celine's Congregation, and her age group, believed me. But, I was elated that Sister Elizabeth Cashman believed me, as she was highly respected in her Community. Now I felt that I could be myself, my whole self.

For the first time in my life, I felt completely assimilated as a survivor of sexual abuse and as a lesbian. I interpreted our conversation that day, and a later discussion, to mean that I would be accepted in the Community with their full knowledge of who I was. I further hoped that the Sisters of Charity of Cincinnati would begin ministering to victims of sexual abuse by priests and sisters, and also to lesbians and gay men.

However, this elation was short-lived, as I was about to allow myself to be victimized by my own naïveté once again.

As a follow-up to this visit with Sister Elizabeth Cashman, I wrote her a long letter thanking her again for listening, witnessing, believing, and offering sympathy. I had heard what I believed was an "apology from you as a representative of the Sisters of Charity."

Then I turned to the other piece of the puzzle that we had never addressed: Why was I "twice asked to leave the Community?" Why was I "banished through the backdoor without saying goodby, which remains an awful embarrassment and trauma for me?"

I mentioned my experience with the mean-spirited Sister Angelica, and my beliefs that she represented woman's inhumanity to women. I asked Sister Elizabeth how she personally "felt" about learning this dark history of Sister Rita Celine and whether she herself needed to further process the experience. In addition and as promised, I sent along information about homosexuality and urged her to integrate it within the College curriculum. After all, Sister Elizabeth was Assistant to the President of the College. I also sent information about Lesbian Sisters, suggesting an educational format for her Congregation.

Soon, I called my long lost friend, Sister Maria Garlock. We met for lunch in Kettering, Ohio the following week. We sat in the garden atmosphere of a popular restaurant. It was so good to be with her.

Then she came to my home for a visit, as I needed to talk, but did not want to discuss sexual abuse in public. When I told Sister Maria that a Sister of Charity had sexually abused me, she inquired if this person was still alive. I said, "No." She fell silent and had nothing more to say. I never went on to identify Sister Rita Celine as the perpetrator because I believed Sister Maria did not want to know something that unpleasant. Moreover, I remembered that when Sister Maria was Principal at Saint Joseph Commercial High School in the mid sixties, while Rita was at South Holland, she had proudly described Sister Rita Celine as her mentor.

Their relationship was never clarified for me, and the few times we met after this visit, Sister Maria carefully avoided the subject, as did I. It was as if she had never heard about my sexual trauma or needed to pretend it never happened for her own peace of mind. She focused on telling me of her ministry at Good Samaritan Hospital, where Sister Rita Celine had also volunteered.

Also, I contacted Sister Jean Therese Durbin, whom I had met in 1966 in Trinidad, Colorado when I had been sent on mission. Sister Jean Therese was proudly from Sun Fish, Kentucky. In 1969, I had visited her in Trinidad where she and two other Sisters had moved out of the St. Joseph Convent and into a home in the parish neighborhood.

These sisters were happy to be living a family style home life. My visit happened to fall on the first anniversary celebration of their move out of the Convent. Jean Therese said they were "Like three pigs in the mud on a sunny day." Our reunion was wonderful.

This was also the first time I saw the Sisters of Charity of Cincinnati's modified habit in person. The material was steel blue, with matching cape and white pointed collar. The headgear or "bonnet" had white trim with blue veil. Some Sisters seemed embarrassed, as the hems were mid calf. I suspect this change was difficult for some. However, Sister Jean Therese seemed to have no trouble adjusting to her hem just below the knee.

Until about 1970, I remained in contact with Sister Jean Therese and, although my net pay was only fifty-four dollars a week, I sent the Trinidad Sisters money to help their ministry with the poor. After Sister Jean Therese left this ministry, we lost track of each other until 1997.

So, with her phone number in hand, I called her in Kettering and was amazed that she lived about two blocks from the office where I now practiced psychotherapy. Our reunion was wonderful, and best of all, Sister Jean Therese invited me to join her as an Associate of the Sisters of Charity of Cincinnati.

This was a new category for lay people that the Congregation had created in the mid 1970's. Indeed, during the next year, 1998, I signed on as an Associate, which I saw as fortuitous and a personal

Godsend. At that time I was caring for my sister Carol who lived only two more years, dying in August 2000.

The Associates and Sisters gave me much needed support during a stressful time. At this point, I strongly believed I was getting more grounded in my spiritual life through the ongoing link with the Sisters of Charity. And, although I had begun to search out parish churches, I still felt no community.

During one of our many visits, I finally told Sister Jean Therese that a Sister of Charity had sexually abused me. We were sitting at a round card table in her apartment that she shared with another Sister. Jean Therese guessed immediately that it was Sister Rita Celine, which I admitted was correct.

At the time, we were paging through the 1996 *Cycle of Life*, a yearly booklet published by the Sisters of Charity of Cincinnati about their deceased Sisters. Jean Therese turned to Sister Rita Celine's page, and pointed to her (Rita). I asked Sister Jean Therese how she guessed, and Jean Therese said, "I just knew". Then she shared a personal secret of her own behavior, as an adult, and said, "You don't seem surprised." Indeed I was not surprised, just stunned, but I chose to say nothing.

I also got in touch with Nancy Bramlage, a Sister of Charity who Rita Celine sponsored for the Convent. During our first visit, Nancy asked, "What ever happened between you and Rita Celine? You were always so close?"

I can't remember what I said or even if I responded. At a later visit, I informed Nancy that a Sister of Charity of Cincinnati had sexually abused me. She asked if my abuser was still living. I said, "No."Nancy did not connect her question of "You and Rita Celine were always so close." with my informing her that I had been sexually abused by a Sister of Charity of Cincinnati who was dead.

HELLO! Nothing more was asked or said.

At this point, May 12, 1998, I received a telephone call from Sister Elizabeth Cashman, which rocked my world.

Two months later, on July 7, I completed writing my response to her call. The issue was that Sister Elizabeth had discovered my "coming out about Rita Celine's sexual abuse" to Sister Maria and Sister Jean Therese, and she needed to question me about my motivation. Her placating comments that I "had a good life" made me feel as if Sister Elizabeth Cashman was once again the Novice Mistress addressing me as a young Postulant.

In her voice I heard, as I explained in writing to her: "Your hand goes up with STOP written on it in yellow, meaning caution, and I should return to my seat and be quiet. I now heard you say 'No' to my Lesbian Sister educational proposals, 'No' to the Gathering, 'No' to the Associate Group, 'No' to my repeating anything more about my story."

On July 7, 1998, I wrote Sister Elizabeth that her May phone call left me shell shocked; I had believed she was receptive and accepting of my offer to send Lesbian Sister information with Sister Maria when she came to Cincinnati [See page 99].

She also seemed to reverse her earlier comment about Sister Rita Celine's not being respected and influential with her Community, and even worse, she implied that my identity as a lesbian was justification for silencing me. I explained that she herself had given me these two old friends phone numbers so that I could communicate with them.

I further wrote that I thought Sister Jean Therese deserved an explanation for my dropping out of her life, hiding my shame, so to speak. In fact, Jean Therese was thankful for my reappearance and relieved that she had not somehow caused my silence. Sister

Maria was an even older friend, dating back to Saint Joseph Commercial High School; moreover, she also had a strong connection with Sister Rita Celine.

During our visit, we remembered going together to Mass at St. Joe's, and shared good relationships with wonderful sisters like Sister Maggie Dee, who urged us to stretch ourselves to better serve people.

Talking to Sister Elizabeth about my personal/spiritual journey was not an attempt to "out" Rita Celine or the Sisters of Charity. For me, these reconnections were necessary because the subject continued to be an unsealed trauma, soothed by conversations with caring friends. I honestly did not see how I could continue my spiritual life within the Community, with a huge part of my history simply erased or left blank. Assimilation requires wholeness and openness, and I was in the middle of this process.

My letter asked Sister Elizabeth if she was denying my right to ever tell the truth. Though she might wish it to be true, my journey with her to Sister Rita Celine's graveside had not erased my experience; the abuse of trust of a fifteen year-old-innocent by a teacher, an elder, a Religious Sister, who is supposed to be chaste and pure, a representative of the Holy Catholic Church.

I reiterated my desire to help the Sisters of Charity of Cincinnati Congregation prevent such recurrences by providing information or personally assisting as a clinical social worker and psychotherapist. To allow me to do so would turn my traumatic crisis into a positive outcome. My hope at this point, was still that Sister Elizabeth would grasp the depth of my need to stay linked with the Sisters of Charity.

Sister Elizabeth's phone call also led me to weigh the proper language of my seduction. Was Rita a pedophile, who preys on elementary aged children or adolescents? Was Rita an institutional lesbian, a heterosexual who behaved as a homosexual because there are no men in the Convent? Was Rita a lesbian? After a decade and a half of psychotherapy, with several therapists at the cost of thousands, I believe that Rita was a sick, sick, sick pedophile regardless if she was a lesbian or not.

Sexual orientation does not equate pedophilia. However, as a would-be progressive Religious Order, Sister Elizabeth's Community could influence the Cincinnati archdiocese to begin programs for gay and lesbian youth to help people become tolerant of others and, perhaps, learn to respect themselves.

This could prevent isolation, depression, broken marriages, and suicides. They also could provide lesbian information and programming within their own Congregation for their lesbian sisters. I wish that I had also suggested it could educate themselves on pedophilia.

I repeated my offer to attend the Gathering, a Congregational event every four years to focus on ideas generated from the Sisters to develop programs for the following four years. In fact, Sister Jean Therese had already invited me to reveal my spiritual journey. Our agreement was that I would talk about my discovery of lesbianism, and my spiritual path, while leaving out my experience of sexual abuse by a Sister.

My epistle to Sister Elizabeth ended by reminding her that my sister and mother were both extremely ill, and I needed to focus on the precious time with them. I informed Sister Elizabeth that I wondered if her call was politically, and not personally motivated, when she said, "I am concerned for you."

I said, "I felt a fear cloud gathering, however, I was no longer afraid."

Looking back, perhaps I should have been afraid. Was Sister

Elizabeth giving me a very clear message that I was to move on, or was she sending a mixed message? She cared about me, but only if I kept silent. Or, had I read too much into her words of acceptance and support? Were she and others beginning to let me know they would close ranks on anything that could hurt the Sisters of Charity of Cincinnati's sanctified reputation: Rita's drinking, her seductions, and the suffering of victims like myself? Was it the practice to suppress all attempts to rectify their Religious Order's injustices? I continued to want to believe these Sisters were spiritually powerful women, not women of power.

Nevertheless, before their actions fully sank in, I loyally continued my attempts to reconnect with them. I truly believed this was my intended spiritual journey. I told myself that I was approaching the pre-Rita dream of being part of a healthy, God-filled Community—the Sisters of Charity of Cincinnati.

For instance, while still working and living in Centerville, I volunteered on Tuesdays to be at the Motherhouse in order to be of service to the retired Sisters. Often I left my home around 6 AM, went to Mass at the Motherhouse, and then began my day of volunteering.

I drove the Sisters shopping, took them to restaurants, to visit family and friends, to the Cincinnati Zoo, and to the Butterfly Museum. I used one of the Community's fleet of cars, gassed full at the Motherhouse's private pump. Sometimes, I spent the night at Seton Hall, which is on the Motherhouse grounds, joined the Sisters at morning Mass, and ate breakfast with them before returning to my home.

Before I could consider becoming an Associate, I needed to find out what was documented about my twice leaving the Postulancy. I called and spoke with a Sister in the Archives located on the Motherhouse grounds. She made me copies from the Community Register. They were waiting at the reception desk on August 11, 1998.

They read that I entered September 8, 1963 and left May 29, 1964; re-entered August 28, 1966 and left February 3, 1967. No reason was given for my leaving. I thought and prayed long and hard for an answer. Then the answer came: Write Sister Emily Anne Phelan. I did so, and Sister said she would be at the Motherhouse. We made arrangements to meet for dinner.

I met Sister Emily Anne at the Motherhouse where we ate in the cafeteria—which we knew as the refectory in 1963. We chose our meal buffet style, still two entrees!

Sister led me to the rear seating; I assume for privacy. It was good to see her. I asked her why I was asked to leave. Her response was, "We were going through so much as a Community with Vatican II." Then she spoke with sadness about some Sisters giving her a hard time when she allowed the Postulants to wear regular clothes on special occasions. (I think she said Easter.) I was left with the impression that I had done nothing wrong, yet something did not ring true. I did not want to believe my feeling that Sister Emily Anne might know something about Sister Rita Celine, or about Rita and myself, so I quickly brushed it aside. I was and I am grateful, and I believed her. She set me free to become an Associate as far as my history of being a Postulant.

However, I still needed to check out any backlash I might experience because of being a lesbian Associate. I contacted Sister Barbara Hagedorn, who was then a Councilor on the Congregational Leadership, directly responsible to the President Sister Mary Ellen Murphy.

Barbara and I were in the Postulancy together in 1966-1967, she was in the East at the Motherhouse, and I in the West in Pueblo,

Colorado. We met in Barbara's office. I told her of my desire to become an Associate, and I wanted to know up front if there would be any difficulty with the fact that I was a lesbian. Barbara responded with what I wanted to hear, and I set the wheels in motion to apply to become an Associate of the Sisters of Charity of Cincinnati.

On October 6, 1998, [See page 98] I innocently wrote to the Sisters to express gratitude for what I saw as my spiritual homecoming. My letter, which was partly printed in the Sisters' *UPDATE*, an internal newsletter, emphasized, beyond gratitude for being an Associate, my desire to promote their potential for helping multicultural people. I proposed a "Day of Reconciliation" at which the Sisters of Charity would publicly acknowledge a *mea culpa* for all the neglects, abuses, etc., delivered by the Catholic Church upon human beings different from the majority.

That part was not reprinted in *UPDATE*, nor was my request for a public apology; a Day of Reconciliation at the Motherhouse was met with profound silence.

In the meantime, I did meet with Sister Elizabeth Cashman several times. On February 18, 1999, [See page 105.] I wrote to her about some of the personal details of my spiritual life, including an account of an experience two years earlier in 1997 when I sat up in bed and heard God say to me, "John Christopher is the One". I expressed concern about finding my Voice and believed God said, "Trust me," and so I did.

I told Sister Elizabeth that I believed she was God's Human Vessel to help me put closure on my Convent years. However, I misinterpreted some of her concern. In July 7, 1998, I felt that I had misjudged Sister Elizabeth when I implied that her concern for me was political, not personal. In order for us to move on, I had to symbolically cut John Christopher, the Novice Mistress representing THE ESTABLISHMENT, loose. (And we did so in the Motherhouse Chapel in 1999, taking rope around each of our wrists, praying over it; then I cut the rope and placed it around a wooden crucifix made from the Motherhouse novice stairs dated 1894-1997.)

In October 2000 [See page 108], I met with Sister Elizabeth. I wanted to share with her the letter that Sister Rita Celine had sent to Carol in 1964. It was not until after Carol's death in August 2000 that I found Rita's letter among my sister's personal papers. I knew that she had saved it for me to read. Finally, in reading it I discovered why, following Rita's death four years before on December 27, 1996, Carol referred to Rita as a "sneaky black rat."

My anger centered on Rita Celine's writing this toxic note to my sister, pulling Carol into her web. It was after a Sunday lunch in the Motherhouse when Sister Elizabeth and I went upstairs— ironically to the same parlor where Mother Mary Omer and I had met in November 1964 to consider my return to the Convent. When I handed Sister Elizabeth Rita's letter to Carol from 1964, she read and reread it, finally expressing anger with Rita that she had broken the Order's procedures in failing to get permission from the Postulant Mistress to visit with me. In Sister Elizabeth's presence, as an act of good faith, I tore up Rita's letter.

Several years later, I would regret this good faith act, as I regretted in the early 1980's tearing up Rita's cryptic prayer cards and notes to me. Out of all of the proof I destroyed, I regret tearing up this letter from Rita to Carol the most because Carol saved it for 38 years. Carol saved it to help me and I destroyed it—I felt somehow I had dishonored her wanting to help me.

Following this visit with Sister Elizabeth, I realized that she said nothing about Rita's impropriety in the letter, Rita's motives, or my feelings. It began to register with me that certain rules were sacred, others were to be never talked about, and "rules" were far more important than one's authentic spiritual journey. However, in the winter of 2006, Sister Elizabeth indirectly gave me a gift that still makes me smile.

My "real life" in the meantime was not going well. Carol and Mom were both seriously ill in 1999. Within two years Carol's diabetes led to blindness, and her early death at age sixty-two. Both she and Mom lived in independent homes, with me as the sole caregiver. My grieving for my beloved sister was blended with caring for Mom. Overwhelmed, I decided to decrease my therapy practice and simplify my life. In March 2001, I sold the building my practice was in, and handed new client referrals to faithful colleagues, some of who had been renters in my building.

This property sale left me with furniture from the practice to donate. As it happened, I saw an ad in the *UPDATE*, requesting donations of furniture. The contact person was Sister Barbara Hagedorn. At that time Barbara was still on the Executive Council of the Leadership of the Sisters of Charity. I called, informing Barbara that I had furniture and that I would be at the Motherhouse in Cincinnati on that particular Tuesday volunteering, and could stop at her office and bring swatches of material for her consideration.

We agreed to meet on April 24, 2001 in what was then Barbara's office. Upon leaving, as I looked out of her window, I noticed construction underway. I inquired, and Barbara said, "That's going to be The Village at Bayley Place, why don't you come?" I had what I call a "spiritual experience." It was as if the Holy Spirit was saying, "Why don't you come?"

It was as if time stood still, and the words were in slow motion. There was complete silence, the room was dazzling white, and I felt suspended in space. I was filled with unconditional peace, hope, and faith. I went across the street to inquire, and found myself putting down a $1,000 deposit on a cottage.

One day in September, I was driving down the sunny, peaceful tree-lined avenue of the Motherhouse. I parked on the side of the building and began unloading items to store in the basement. Sister Barbara had made arrangements for me to leave some of my personal property until I could move them into my cottage at The Village at Bayley Place. A Sister yelled out the window that the Twin Towers had been hit by a plane. I was invited into the Sisters' Community Room to watch the news.

An elderly Sister said in response to the newscaster, "We should not be surprised. Osama bin Laden has been warning us for six months that a terrorist attack would happen on American soil." We went to the Motherhouse chapel to pray. We were all in acute shock, and anguish, as was our nation.

Because of 9/11, life became surreal and seemed to be spinning out of control. I felt I needed to set my roots at The Village at Bayley Place sooner than planned. Initially, I deliberately chose the two bedroom end unit model, which would not be available for two years, because I wanted more time to be sure I was making the right decision with my reconnection to the Sisters of Charity.

With the money from the sale of my office building, I conveniently had the assets for the purchase. Investing in it would mean living on, and in, property owned by the Sisters of Charity of Cincinnati. I had planned to move when I reached the required admission age of sixty.

I received a call from the Coordinator at the Village who informed me that I could move in earlier than expected. For me it was the providential card; I believed this was God's will that I was able to move into my cottage sooner. I would barely be fifty-eight, but was told that I was close enough in age.

I thought "What about my clients?" I had kept a few clients I had been working with for some years. And what about my personal mail during this transition? The Sister running the Sisters of Charity post office informed me I could have a mailbox on the grounds of the Motherhouse. A colleague offered space in her Centerville, Ohio office on Saturdays, so I continued working with my established clients. Rumor was that because of 9/11, there were cancellations at the cottages, but I never gave this a thought, as I believed this was God's will for me. Because all of the logistical details seemed to be resolved, I felt this was providential, and I prepared to move, which took from January to April 2002.

In the midst of my moving, my Mom had a massive heart attack, so I began driving back and forth between Cincinnati and Dayton. Physical therapy in the nursing home helped Mom regain some strength, but when her discharge team met with us, they made it clear that she could not return to her home. I had an Occupational Therapist evaluate Mom's home. Her opinion was that it would not be safe for Mom to return.

The choices they gave were that Mom could remain there, or move in with me. On July 19, 2002, I picked Mom up from the nursing home in a wheelchair, because it was evident that she could never walk on her own again. Mom came to live with me at Bayley Place. Although she received physical therapy in my home, as I wanted her to have hope, I knew we all were just going through the motions.

I found great joy in the belief that I was reconnecting and spiritually belonging to the Sisters of Charity, excited that if my Mom lived long enough, I could continue to care for her in my beautiful, handicapped accessible home.

If she needed nursing home care, the Sisters of Charity owned a home right up the street on the Bayley Place property. I also appreciated having a direction that would help my retirement plans, and was grateful to complete the damaged circle that had been interrupted by Sister Rita Celine's relationship, which I had felt was somehow connected to my two rejections earlier by this Community. Regardless of how I had felt, I convinced myself that the facts of the archives search removed this concern.

I was regaining trust in myself, and with that trust came a deeper spiritual life. I increasingly wanted people to know who I am, which included my history, and that meant that if they befriended me they got the whole package. No more secrets!

By 2002, eighteen Sisters of Charity knew that I was sexually abused. Some knew that Sister Rita Celine was the perpetrator. Some promised to pray for me; a few urged more psychotherapy.

One said, "You came down here to put all this behind you, and now you are telling." Another said I was crazy; yet another said I only wanted money. Another Sister accused me of being a liar; another said I got involved with Rita because I was a lesbian and so there was no sexual abuse; another implied I got involved with Rita because my Mom did not express affection easily. This Sister did not even know my mother.

However, some Sisters believed me and most urged me to speak with their President and Executive Council. I was weighing all of this, but first I wanted to talk with my old friend Sister Maggie Dee, former Principal at St. Joe's High School.

I visited Sister Maggie Dee at Mother Margaret Hall, an assisted and nursing care facility for the Sisters on the Motherhouse grounds. We discussed life philosophies, religions, Thomas Merton, and we shared fond memories of St. Joe's High School. I revealed to her that a Sister of Charity had sexually abused me while I was in high school.

Sister Maggie Dee did not bat an eye, said nothing, and hung her head. I believe that at that meeting she had a realization—she knew who the abuser was. We both sat quietly, and without saying anything else, said goodbye for the last time. Shortly after this meeting, Maggie Dee died.

Business card and street sign from my
practice in Dayton, Ohio.

October 6, 1998

Dear Sisters,

I have recently been accepted as an Associate in Mission. I attended the Easter Network meeting on Saturday, October 3, 1998, and I thank you for your welcoming and kindness expressed to me there. I feel it was a spiritual homecoming for me personally, a sense of belonging, a connecting with powerful women of God, not women of power.

I am grateful for you inviting me to your table and by doing so we all shared at the Lord's Table. One Body, One Blood = enfleshed and inclusive. The experience was profound at a very holy place, the Motherhouse.

Good things are happening, brighter days are here. Like a line in the movie 'Field of Dreams': "If you build it, they will come." So I say to you, if you keep processing all that I experienced October 3rd, you will not have to worry about vocations. If you openly offer and accept, they will come, i.e., multi-cultural people. Before that, however, and if I may make a suggestion, a working enfleshed definition of "multi-cultural" needs to be in place. And coming from that definition, a Day of Reconciliation needs to be offered whereby the Sisters of Charity (S.C.) will publicly acknowledge a mea culpa for all the neglects, abuses, etc. delivered by the Catholic Church upon human beings different from the majority. You, the S.C., can be that enfleshed vessel, that holy vehicle to bring about healing.

We, multi-cultural people, are standing in the shadows waiting to hear an apology from the Church before we can accept and move forward. We are forgiving people, but we need to hear a public apology. We will come; offer a Day of Reconciliation at your Motherhouse.

I thank you for listening.

Linda Mahlmeister

I wrote to the Sisters of Charity of Cincinnati expressing my appreciation, and offered some suggestions as an Associate. Parts of the letter were printed in their UPDATE periodical.

July 07, 1998

Dear Sister Elizabeth,

I am writing in response to our telephone conversation of Tuesday, May 12, 1998. This effort comes with an act of faith that I want to believe your concern for me is genuine and not politically motivated. I want you to know that if I have misjudged your intention, I apologize and will do so directly to you. Regardless, please indulge me by reading this letter

Let me begin by responding to what I believe I heard you say to me. Paraphrasing you...."you tell me you came to the Mount to put closure on your convent years and then you have come out to Sr Jean Therese and Sr Maria. You know Sr Rita Celine has been influential to Sr Maria and to the Dayton Community I am concerned for you" And I heard myself saying to you "I think it's about belonging or I want to belong" [this was the 1st time I put these feelings into words] and that I needed to process it and we agreed that I needed to process it and that I would call you in July Then, I believe you said "You have a good life" and I felt dismissed and remember saying that "I'm going to work real hard at not taking this as a rejection" I don't remember any more as I began to fade. (Clinically, a re-enactment phase began. Your call threw me back to the trauma of being asked to leave the Community twice - of being rejected with no reason given).

When you said "You have a good life", I felt your hand go up with STOP (written on it in YELLOW) and for me to return to my seat and be quiet (I became young - a Postulant and you were Sr John Christopher, the Novice Mistress). I heard you say NO.

- No to the Gathering
- No to the Associates Group
- No to saying anything more about my story

Again, when you said "You have a good life" I thought to myself, I know I have a good life, but what does that have to do with spiritually belonging, which is the only thing that I feel is lacking in my life ? Then I thought, maybe you think I want to return to the convent. I assure you I do not want to - I just want to connect and spiritually belong. For two (2) days after our

1

telephone conversation of May 12, I walked around shell-shocked. I thought, on one hand Sr

Elizabeth was receptive and accepted my offer of sending Lesbian Nun (LN) information with

Sr Maria and then on the other hand I see STOP in YELLOW   =CAUTION=. This remains

crazy-making for me - like an elephant in the living room that no one acknowledges. They just

walk around it. I wish you would have asked to see me instead of using the distance the

telephone offers. I do much better face to face.

Now, I do not understand your "concern" for me and your comment regarding Rita being

well-respected and influential in the Dayton area. God knows, I have known this for years! I

have come to the realization that this is exactly why I did not come out until after her death. I

mean, who would believe a Lesbian who was thrown out of SC twice compared to a PILLAR of

the SC Community and the Dayton Community? And, that Rita has influenced Maria? But, what

does this fact of Rita's influence have to do with my life NOW? As I mentioned to you, I am no

longer afraid. However, your comment could be interpreted as   I am supposed to be afraid. I

feel there is a "fear cloud" and it's not about <u>my</u> fear   I am not getting it. However, I have been

told that I am naive. I hope someday you clarify this for me.

I want to put my recall of <u>events in context leading up to our May 12th conversation</u>.

1 Why did I come out to Sr Jean Therese - to share my journey, to explain what

caused me to drop out of her life for 30 years. I am glad that I have done this because Jean

stated she felt she had done something to offend me and caused my disappearance.

2. Why did I come out as a Lesbian and as sexual abuse survivor of a Nun to Sr Maria

- even though our time frame was not the same at St. Joseph Commercial HS, she and I had a

connectedness there of which I also have fond memories of the spirit of the school, of going to

mass at St. Joe's , of some wonderful Sr of Charity like Maggie Dee (Magdeline Delores) who

believed in me to be a better person, to stretch myself and be of service to people.

3. I have a right to tell my personal/spiritual journey In June, 1997, I told you what I

said to you was confidential and what I mean is there is no need to "out Rita or the Sisters of

Charity", and that remains my position. However, what remains important is that this trauma was

2

done to me (not who did it) and it is healing for me to talk about it. If people put 2 & 2 together and ask me, was Rita the one or was the person a Sister of Charity, then, these are the options that I have available to me:

- lie about it;
- tell the truth; or
- be evasive and avoidant.

I ask your direction as a person of God and a Sister of Charity regarding what my response needs to be. My preference is ....

History:

1. In June, 1997, we went to Rita's grave to:

- Put closure on my convent years - I believe I have done this.
- Put closure on being sexually abused - I have come to realize that a trip to the Mount will never erase my indelible scar   I am not one to rationalize the sin and crime that was done to me nor the abuse of trust held by a 15-year-old toward my teacher or my innocence of Faith in God that was damaged by Rita's manipulative denial of her own problem(s).

2. In February, 1998, I got a telephone call from a priest who asked me to befriend a SC and a Lesbian Nun. This person is identified which caused me to meet with you a second time to seek direction and both of us agreed I was not the person to help   . However, we both got into indirectly helping   . Now here is an issue that I have always had ... is this providential, and God's will that I do something about this situation? Admittedly, you informed me there was nothing to offer   in your Community, and in fact went outside your Community to another religious order to get LN information.

Motivation

So, to make it short, I got into gathering information about LNs and offered to you and the SCs my professional services as a clinical social worker, psychotherapist, former member of the SCs, and a Lesbian, for what I sincerely believe are the following motivations:

3

- to have a positive outcome of what was the #1 most traumatic experience of my life, i.e. Rita and her sexual abuse of me.

- to come full circle (Linda-Rita-   ) to indirectly help   instead of a payback to her and   " for what I perceive of her as mistreatment of me where I tried to get in contact with Rita around 1982 and confront her (Rita). So, I began by gathering LN information so hopefully the information could find its way to   .

- for the common good of all LN of the Sisters of Charity who are crying out silently to be accepted, to get on with inclusiveness, with stopping the suffering, with having potential positive energies being realized instead of the exclusive, closeted negative energies which cause ongoing suffering and erode the Whole, the common good, the higher purpose I still believe we are placed on this earth to help fulfill. My journey has brought me to a place where I want to reach out to these LNs.

- I continue to care and respect the Sisters of Charity

One of your sisters told me, "our Community has had two human sexuality programs offered." My response is--any educator can teach Human Sexuality/Sexual Orientation issues, but homophobia needs to be addressed by a homosexual because we understand, work daily with the issues of internalized homophobia as well as with societies homophobia and this is about emotions/feeling of fear which need to be processed, not taught.

I offered my professional services to do a program (not for the general Congregation) but for some Nuns that you would hand-pick. People in leadership, Nuns who are sincerely interested in helping their religious order and their Sisters of Charity to become inclusive and more healthy The statistic is that homosexuals are 10% of any population, so why would there be a different statistic in the SC?

4

- hopefully for a religious order (you folks) to influence the Cincy archdiocese to begin programs for Gay/Lesbian youth in parochial schools, parishes, and other religious orders to help young people realize who they are so they will not be prey to a LN, gay priest or brother or homosexual laity; to prevent isolation, depression, suicide, broken marriages and families, etc. etc. etc.!!!

Spiritual Belonging

I had indicated to you in a previous telephone conversation, that I was on a journey to spiritually connect i.e. checking out local parishes - and here again is where I believe I got clouded in my providential belief system (i.e. God is present in human experience) and I think several issues are operating in a timely fashion.

- that the Gathering event for the 1st time had a program for lay women to share their spiritual journey
- Sr Jean invited me to come to the gathering, informing me of her belief that my spiritual journey has value and would be helpful to the Sr of Charity (except leave out sexual abuse part).
- That the time is now to tell my story vs. when will there be a time, as the Gathering will not be held again for several years.
- A way for me to connect and spiritually belong.

Present

I am facing the fact that there are going to be lots of "passing on" of people I dearly love and respect, and, yes, myself and my generation will be stepping up to the plate to "carry on" before we "pass on" If, in the last four (4) months, you have picked up on any intensity in my mood or behavior this is the reason. I feel loved-ones will be dying, I feel time is running out, I'm scared, and I feel an urgency and want to connect/belong.

5

- Knowledge of realizing that I need to face the fact that my mother is 84 and not in good physical health, that my 60-year-old diabetic sister is going blind and will never reach 84, and the awesome realization that I have total responsibility for these two people, living alone in their independent homes. These people are all the family I have.

- Jean's one lung is not functioning adequately, and is on oxygen. Thirty-three years have gone by since we initially met and 30 years have been wasted through my "dropping out"

I know God loves me! I truly believe I would not be alive if my God did not love me. He walked with me even when I rejected/abandoned Him.

I thank you for our phone conversation May 12, 1998, as I did not realize the depth of the need I have in looking at my "belonging issue" I only have shades of it, no concrete answers yet.

Best regards,

Working to Make It Happen

Members of the Gathering/Chapter planning committee and facilitators have been meeting since August to prepare for the event. From left to right are: (seated) Sisters Elizabeth Cashman and Nancy Bramlage; (standing) S. Carol Wirtz, facilitators Jean Alvarez and S. Nancy Conway, and Sisters Mary Bookser, Betty Finn and Barbara Hagedorn.

8   *Intercom*

Members of the Sisters of Charity of Cincinnati Chapter Committee. The Chapter, or Gathering, takes place every four years. The main purpose is to plan their missions for the next four years.

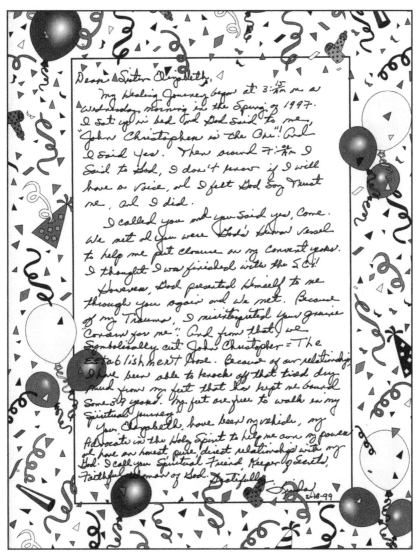

Ttranscription of the letter on the following page.

Transcription of my letter to Sister Elizabeth Cashman from the previous page.

Dear Sister Elizabeth,

My Healing Journey began at 3:15 am on a Summer morning in 1997. I sat up in bed and God said to me, "John Christopher is the One." and I said Yes. Then around 7:00 am, I said to God, I don't know if I will have a Voice. Amd I felt God say, "trust me." And I did.

I called you and you said yes, come. We met and you were God's Human Vessel to help me put closure on my Convent years.

I thought I was finished with the SC's! However, God presented Himself to me through you again, and we met. Because of my Trauma I misinterpreted your genuine "concern of me." And from that concern we symbolically cut John Christohper —THE ESTABLISHMENT—loose.

Because of our relationship, I have been able to knock off that tired dry mud from my feet that kept me bound for some 39 years. My feet are free to walk in my spiritual journey.

You, Elizabeth, have been my vehicle, my advocate in the Holy Spirit to help me own my power and have an honest, pure, direct relationship with my God. I call you Friend, Keeper of Secrets, Faithful Woman of God.

Gratefully,

Linda

2-18-99

941 Valla View
Cincinnati, OH 45238

CINCINNATI OH
DEC 19
PM
2000

Ms. Linda Mahlmeister
5515 Paddington Road
Centerville, OH 45459

May the
Wonder and Joy & peace
of the Season
stay with you
through the year

Dear Linda,
    I am thinking of you
during this season I know
you are missing your sister
& sorrowing to see your mother
fail I am praying for you.
        Love,
        Elizabeth

A Christmas message from Elizabeth Cashman, SC, acknowledging the death of my sister, Carol, and my Mom's declining health.

October 27, 00

Dear Elizabeth,

I was not feeling well Sunday. Three days in the Rose Room was too
much for me! Then sharing Rita's note _{& CAROL} with you - I feel Rita wasn
even toxic with my Sister, pulling Carol also into Rita's Web.
I am angry and resent her doing this.

I than had a re-enactment phase occur in your presence. (I began
flooding and having flashbacks.) I felt fear. I felt you were somehow
going to harm me, although I intellectually, emotionally and spiritually know you would never do this. I had to check out that you
are a straight (Heterosexual) nun as I am not strong enough to
befriend a Lesbian nun, especially one who is in Rita's age group.
Secondly, I trusted the "God is Love" Rita, and look what happened
to me. I pray I did not insult/offend you. Please let me know if
I did.

I felt evil was present, Satan himself..I know that feeling well
when he is present and I experience the same occurrence. It goes
like this.- I am in an airplane heading for the ground. The plane
is shaking and the windows are cracking and I am trying to pull the
plane up to prevent crashing. I am trapped. I am internally
crying out but nobody hears me because I do not have a voice.
My Soul is on fire but nobody sees me, nobody sees my pain. the end.
I really tried to regain my composure in your presence but I could not
I just could not. I am sorry. I hope I did not scare you.
Please let me know if I did.

-2-

Sunday was suppose to be two Friends coming together to share
Life's happenings and to share my progress, and it turned into a
nightmare. Since June, I looked so forward to telling you of my
spiritual progress. I became overwhelmed with fear and despair.
After our visit, I feel I have spent days in Hell, but I have not drank
I refuse to let Rita once again have my Soul through such destructive
behavior.

The timing of all of this is difficult. I have enough to deal with
in Carol's death. Grieving my loss, grieving my mother's loss.
At this point, it is unbearable pain to realize my Mom will be passing
on. I will have no more Family.

It is important to me that you understand me, where I am coming from -
where I have been
thus the enclosed PTSD info.

I hope you have had a relaxing, fun time at CTA and heard
Jeannine Gramick.

Love,
Linda

*A letter to Elizabeth Cashman, SC, regarding my shock about about Rita Celine's
letter to my sister, Carol.*

Left to Right: Jean Therese Durbin, SC; Mary Ann Humbert, SC, Director of Associates; and me at Paddington House, August 2000.

Right: Christmas note from Nancy Bramlage, SC.

Dear Linda,

Christmas is love
sent from Heaven to earth,
and shared from heart to heart.

I am very grateful that our lives have once again intersected and that we've been able to share in each other's journeys of life and faith. Many blessings on you and and your mom. Love,
Nancy

A gathering of Associates and Sisters of Charity before dinner in my home. Back row third from left: Jean Therese, SC and Nancy Bramlage, SC; seated in armchair right, Diana Bode, SC.

The Call - S. Nancy Bramlage

By Josh Zeller, Communications intern

The decision to pursue a religious vocation is itself a difficult one to make, but for S. Nancy Bramlage, there was a further complication: she had to choose between more than one congregation. Unlike many of her fellow women religious, S. Nancy's first exposure to religious life was not with the Sisters of Charity, but with the Sisters of Notre Dame de Namur.

"I was, as many of us have been, a product of Catholic education," Sister relates. Growing up in Dayton, Ohio, her family attended the Holy Family parish church and schools, for 12 years, she was taught by the Notre Dame Sisters. Her love of learning and the kindness of her teachers instilled in her a desire to teach " I was never one to not want to go to school in the morning; I always wanted to go to school! We played school, too—I was the teacher of my two little brothers!" This game of school among her siblings foreshadowed the career in education that she would begin years later

When she was a little bit older, she also considered motherhood, or working in an orphanage, because she loved children, and had had good experiences babysitting for her neighbors. By her senior year of high school, however, religious life seemed to rise above all other options, and began to call her name. At that time, S. Nancy recalls thinking, "You know, that's a beautiful thing, to be able to give your life over to God " She wanted to give back to God what God had given to her

She approached the pastoral minister for Holy Family, who worked with teenagers in the parish, and told him about her new conviction. "Good," he responded. "Don't go to the [SNDs]." Instead, he wanted to introduce her to the Sisters of Charity A little stunned, S. Nancy agreed, and soon met S Rita Celine Weadick, who at that time was teaching at St. Joseph Commercial High School in Dayton

S. Nancy was not wholly unfamiliar with the Congregation at that time, as her older sister was a student at St. Joseph Commercial, training to become a secretary. "... [S]he went to St. Joseph and loved the Sisters of Charity, and talked about them all the time—how much fun they were," S. Nancy remembers. After she went with S. Rita Celine to visit the Mount St. Joseph Motherhouse, she had to concur with her sister· " .. I came and I found them very friendly"

Yet, this was not enough to make her rule out the Notre Dame Sisters. While S. Nancy found that they were more serious and formal than fun and friendly, these were women that she knew very well, who had been constant figures in her life. Matters were further complicated when S. Nancy's aunt asked her to visit the Benedictine Sisters in Northern Kentucky, a community her aunt knew and loved Three choices loomed before her

Fairly quickly, Sister ruled out the Benedictines. She saw that, while they had ministries, they spent most of their life cloistered in the monastery—this was not something that interested her It was again down to the Notre Dames and the Charities, and neither was so easy to rule out.

But, what S. Nancy found alluring in the Sisters of Charity, besides their loving kindness, was their newness to her life, the fact that they were unexplored ground—"I guess there is part of me that's adventuresome ...," Sister imparts. Correlating too with her sense of adventure was the variety of ministries that Sisters of Charity took on, and around the world—though she wanted to be a teacher, the Notre Dame Sisters focused almost solely on education, and the presence of multiple options was attractive to S. Nancy.

She made her decision. on September 8, 1962, she entered the Sisters of Charity S. Nancy affirms, " .. I just thought, 'I like these Sisters, and I like their spirit,' . [T]hat's what brought me here "

Nancy Bramlage, SC meets Sister Rita Celine as a teenager as told years later.

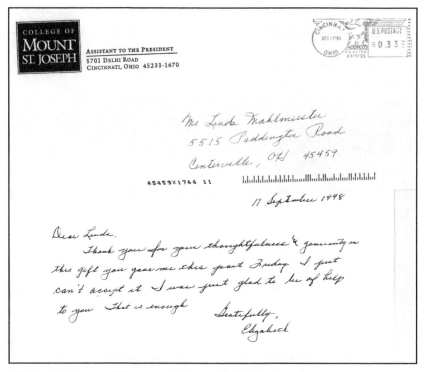

Elizabeth Cashman, SC, returned a financial gift I had sent her.

"You've got to go out and kick ass."

— Maya Angelou

CHAPTER SEVEN

REALITY CHECK, MORE TRAUMA

It was 2003 when I found the courage to address the Executive Council as a group. The Sisters of Charity of Cincinnati's Executive Council in 2003 to 2011 consisted of Sister Barbara Hagedorn, President, and Councilors, Sisters Nancy Bramlage, Georgia Kitt, Mary Michele Fischer, and Maureen Heverin (who was later replaced by Sister Lois Jean Goettke in the spring of 2007) and secretary Sister Patricia Miersberger.

I was an Associate of the Order, and prayed for guidance about how to proceed with divulging the secrets of Sister Rita Celine's sexual abuse. At this time, in addition to the eighteen Sisters of Charity, three Associates also knew of my sexual abuse. I believed that the support of these individual Sisters of Charity would aid me in representing my "story" or "case." I expected them to say in public what they said to me privately—or at least they would write letters of support.

In August, I called Sister Barbara Hagedorn, President, and had my friend, Sister Diana Bode, praying with me during this call. When Sister Barbara answered the phone and heard me ask for an appointment with the Council, she insisted on knowing the nature of the meeting. I said, "It is personal."

Sister Barbara said, "I must know the purpose of your request as the Council is very busy." She frostily refused to schedule Council time, though she was willing to schedule an individual appointment with me, which I was relieved to take. I had mixed feelings, yet felt an individual appointment was better than none.

My head was spinning. My breathing was labored, and my heart felt as if it might explode. Clearly, I was still a prisoner of my history with female authority figures—and Barbara is younger than I am.

I asked two friends to go with me, Sisters Jean Therese Durbin and Elizabeth Cashman. They both declined, which did not bode well. Sister Jean Therese's refusal especially hurt me. Could it have been about her guilt around the confidence she had shared in 1997? She hurt me by saying that the reason I became involved with Rita Celine was because she was a mother substitute. I, of course, responded that Rita Celine had a history of sexual abuse and was an alcoholic, so there could be no excuse for the enabling and co-opting silence of a Sister of Charity.

In September 2003, I went alone to meet Sister Barbara. She greeted me cordially and we sat next to each other. She became chilly as I recounted the history of Sister Rita Celine's sexual abuse. Sister Barbara appeared visibly upset, got up and stood behind her desk, grabbing a bottle of water. I asked if she was all right. She brusquely told me "We are not here to discuss my feelings." She told me she would talk to the Council and call me sometime later. That was all.

Sister Barbara did not get back to me for over a month, nor did anyone from the Council contact me. I was disappointed by her call when she explained that the Council would not let me address them. I wondered if this could have anything to do with Sister Rita Celine's preparation of Sister Nancy Bramladge for the Sisters of Charity back in 1962.

I was joy-filled to become an Associate, live in Bayley Place and walk the holy grounds of the Motherhouse. I truly believe God gave me these gifts to continue to nourish my soul and to be of service to the Sisters of the Motherhouse, and to Mother Margaret Hall. Also, to have a beautiful, peaceful place to care for my Mom was a wonderful gift.

However, within the year of our meeting, the wagons circled around the Sisters of Charity, their defenses were in motion and the shunning began. When I first moved to Bayley Place, I would take the Sisters out to eat, to the movies, to the Zoo, visit with them, and listen to their stories. I also took Lucy, my dog, for a little one-on-one pet therapy when the Sisters would give her treats. I was honored to bring Holy Communion to the Sisters at Mother Margaret Hall. Soon, the Sisters were not available for outings, or visits with Lucy or me.

Although I continued to have friends of the Sisters of Charity and Associates visit me, I became isolated. I would be on my back porch, or look out my kitchen window, and across the street were the Congregational Leadership offices where we meet. I had to have "custody of the eyes" just to cope in my own home. I felt alone in my grief, despair, and disillusion.

My depression, anxiety, and rage deepened. I was responsible for my Mom. I was losing my grip caring for her, and I felt a frantic desperation. I had to make the painful decision to get out of this toxic environment and move to Florida, giving up on my dream of working on my spiritual life at the Motherhouse. For me, this was the third time I was robbed of my spiritual journey.

I felt I had no recourse but to state my feelings in writing to the Executive Council. My feelings of outrage at the betrayal and hypocrisy of the Community were reflected in the letter I wrote to each member of the Council. (I think dated December 13, 2004. Unfortunately, I tore up my copy of this letter).

I could not fathom how a supposed charitable organization, devoted to good works, could treat anyone the way I was being treated—shunned as if I was a leper. In the letter, I summarized the impasse and proposed three remedies to the Council.

First, the Congregation could design a prayer card for victims of abuse. Second, they might prepare a weekend retreat on sexual abuse through the Motherhouse's Spirituality Center, and/or sponsor a talk by Jim Mueller, M.D., then president of the Voice of the Faithful.

Voice of the Faithful is a group initially created by Catholic lay people to give support to those sexually abused by Roman Catholic priests; they later extended their outreach to those sexually abused by Religious Women. Their motto is, "Keep the Faith. Change the Church."

I also reminded the Council that I was invited in 1998 to become a Sisters of Charity Associate, and in 2001 Barbara Hagedorn had invited me to invest in their new residential complex, The Village at Bayley Place (though she later denied issuing the invitation).

Third, I asked for a public apology within the Sisters of Charity Community for my sexual abuse.

Sister Barbara and her Executive Council were neither responsive nor empathetic to my pleas for support, nor did they respond to my letter. I will never forget their self-serving behavior, and I am trying to forgive them, but mostly I blame myself for impotent attempts to reach these women who did not deserve my trust. I expected honor, ethics and kindness, not enabling silence and sophisticated game playing designed to defuse my search for justice.

With my Post Traumatic Stress Disorder (PTSD) increasing, I decided to move to Florida. With the help of friends, I moved Mom to Ft. Myers in a wheelchair on an airplane. She had never flown before. I knew Ft. Myers from yearly visits to Carmen Rosa's home.

Earlier in life, I had promised Mom I would care for her, that she would never have to go into a nursing home, which she called a "County old folks home." To myself, I added, I would care for Mom as long as I could transfer her to and from the wheelchair. I did so from July 19, 2002 until October 22, 2005.

I had Hospice in my home and in October 2005, right before Hurricane Wilma hit Ft. Myers on October 24, 2005, a nurse told me Mom was dying. Mom was immediately transported to Hospice. After eleven days, I was informed Mom had improved and needed to be moved to a nursing home. I asked about the residential wing at Hospice and was informed there was a room available, but it was private pay.

I made arrangements for Mom and she had a lovely, private room, large enough for a pull out bed so I could stay overnight, and a beautiful flowered private porch. The staff who cared for Mom were angels. Mom remained at hospice until she died.

In May 2007 it became obvious that Mom's days were numbered. I asked her if she wanted a Mass of Christian Burial. Mom said, *"No, I don't want a pedophile priest praying over me."* How very sad! This was my Mother's ending after all she gave to the church. She died May 20, 2007.

In September of 2006, I received word indirectly that the President would like me to contact her. On September 2, 2006, [See page 147] I sent Sister Barbara a letter trying to accept her feelings as well as restating my need for some redress. By this time, I had sold my home at Bayley Place, loosing sizable money due to the penalty clause for breaking the lifetime contract. I found it impossible to live on the grounds of a Congregation that was openly shunning me.

Also, Sisters of Charity friends that were aware of the shunning urged me to request financial reimbursement. Refer to letters of support dated July 29, 2004 [See page 136], August 10, 2005 [See page 144], August 11,2005 [See page 142], and February 21, 2006 [See page 145].)

In response to my letter, I received two letters dated November 13, 2006 [See page 149] and February 1, 2007 [See page 150] from Sister Barbara saying that a Sister from a Dominican order, "part of a larger group addressing complaints against Sisters," would meet with me. In the spring of 2007 (I believe it was March 14), still with great fear for obvious reasons, I met with Sister Pat at Crown Plaza Hotel conference room in Fort Myers, Florida. I told her my story.

At the end of our interview, I asked Sister Pat if she had ever interviewed a lesbian. She stated this was her first time. I asked if she ever interviewed a person alleging sexual abuse by a Religious Woman. She stated that I was her first person (so much for firsts!). I also asked Sister Pat how she knew Sister Barbara Hagedorn. She said, "She is a member of the Leadership Conference of Women Religious (LCWR)."

Although I felt she believed me, I also felt that Sister Pat was sending me a message, once again, that I should just put this all behind me. Four months after this meeting, hearing nothing from the leadership, I learned from my friend Sister Dee Sizler that Sister Pat had met briefly with Sister Barbara, and that my case was still under review. I concluded that the meeting with Sister Pat had been another ruse.

It was now blatantly clear that the Sisters of Charity of Cincinnati's leadership, some of its members, as well as the broader Church, hoped that by ignoring me, I would disappear. There would be no accountability, no justice, no apology, and no ministering or compassion. (Refer to letters dated October 11, 2007 [See page 151] and January 12, 2008 [See page 152].

In my maturity and in preparing this book, I have most fully realized the shape of my past. Over the years, I have met other victims of sexual abuse, and, as we compared experiences and insights, I have been literally brought to my knees. The pain and the weight of the life changing experience is, for many victims, at times almost unbearable. But, at last I could see and also understand my passivity.

For years, as an adult, I understood and had faced the sexual abuse, but somehow did not recognize the seductive plot woven by Sister Rita Celine. I can never know whether her scheme was fully conscious, and because it was so veiled, starting with genuine innocence, I cannot even now discern exactly how it turned into something so dark. I never experienced a physical attack known as rape, but was cleverly, cunningly invited to enter a special sexual relationship with all the trappings of seduction.

Sexual abuse is not merely about two people having genital contact. It is always about one person claiming power over another. The adult has social authority, esteem, respect, frequently the power of threat, and is one hundred percent responsible for what unfolds.

Quite often, there is a slow deliberate seduction. They choose their victims wisely and carefully, and then they plot, plan, woo, disguise and, in the end, get their victim. I compare this to where a snake slinks along, watching its victim with the anticipatory advantage of knowing when to attack. It bides its time until its action will be successful.

Victims of sexual abuse feel shame because the sexual activities include elements of physical and psychological pleasure, which leads the victim later to feel somehow responsible for allowing the abuse to happen.

But, the victim has no perspective, or knowledge of choice, or reference point to comprehend what is really going on. She is trapped in her familiar naiveté and trust. She sees herself as powerless, which she is, so she unthinkingly complies.

At the time, this relationship may temporarily give her a sense of being newly in control of her life. Later when the victim realizes she has been abused, she or he feels stupid, embarrassed, duped. She feels rage toward the perpetrator, fears ridicule from others, and anticipates possibly being treated as if she were somehow "damaged goods."

The perpetrator has warned that breaking silence will bring awful consequences from family, friends, and society. In effect, the victim should deny the sexual imposition as though it never occurred, thus rendering it impossible for her to validate her feelings of abuse. She lives in two worlds, one with her external reality, and one with her internal pain, deep sense of betrayal, and fractured self image.

Sister Rita Celine had told me that our intimacy must remain "private." This privacy flattered me, and, in my blindness, allowed the sexual abuse to continue for far too long. I still don't know exactly what her sponsorship for the Convent really meant, but at the time it created fear, in the sense that I believed her when she said my future was in her hands.

I knew that my family would not support me in a public confession. There was a family history of sexual deceit. At age eleven Carol was sexually attacked by a man while delivering newspapers. She came home crying and told Mom, who forced her to be secretive about the episode. The man was not reported to the police. Our brother just took over the newspaper route. Our father was not told, and Carol forever lived with shame and guilt that she was somehow responsible for this attack.

First my sister was attacked, then I was, and each of us was damaged by a family policy of secrecy. Our traumas made it impossible for either of us to know what life would have been like without sexual abuse. My sister's episode was brief, but she moved out at eighteen and never married. I somehow went on, trying to fit into a society that did not, until now, know me. Today I recognize that I was totally isolated. All my usual supports were not available to me about sexual abuse—my family, the religious community, the church.

Why has the story of sexual abuse by Religious Women never been publically told? Why did Catholics and non-Catholics allow these unspoken words and permit the silence to continue regarding sexual abuse by Religious Women? Why can we accept evil behavior from males, but not females?

Priests' sexual abuse is now public knowledge, and some victims have been compensated. If we also accept the hard truth that some Religious Women of the world have abused young people physically, emotionally, sexually, and spiritually, are we challenging motherhood, apple pie, and the American flag? Because of years of cover-up, the mere fact of accusing Religious Women of sexual abuse is like trespassing on sacred ground. Are we trying to preserve a vision of the Virgin Mary?

Someone once said that this scandal should be revealed simply because "I just don't expect it from women; I can't imagine a woman behaving that way." And so, the greater question is raised about the gender double standard. Why is it easier to remove Religious Males from their pedestals than their female counterparts? Beyond that unfathomable mystery, why have women's religious orders not come forth and publicly called to task those who commit and cover up sexual abuse in their own ranks? Why are they enablers and gatekeepers?

A woman I met in 2007, through Voice of the Faithful, has a database of over 400 victims of abuse by Sisters. I am left wondering if this is perhaps the tip of the iceberg. The Roman Catholic Church, through its silence, has failed not only these victims, but has tainted its message of faith, all in its effort to preserve its image and its vast financial holdings.

In 2004, I met with a priest in of Archdiocese of Cincinnati regarding my sexual abuse. After he stated that he was sorry and would pray for me, he informed me that no Archdiocese had any authority over any Religious Women's Congregation.

connection

SISTERS OF CHARITY EMPLOYEE NEWSLETTER

Summer 2003

Sisters of Charity Executive Council 2003-2007

By Mary Kay Gilbert

As reported earlier, the Sisters of Charity of Cincinnati held elections for president and councilors during Chapter in March. The new leadership officially took office July 1, the start of the new fiscal year. The installation ceremony occurred on July 6, with Sisters, Associates and families of the new officers in attendance.

Most employees are already familiar with the new president, S. Barbara Hagedorn. Many know S. Maureen Heverin, who was re-elected to a second term. But three of the councilors have not lived in Cincinnati recently. Here's a chance to learn a little about the 2003-2007 Sisters of Charity of Cincinnati Executive Council.

S. Barbara Hagedorn, president

S. Barbara Hagedorn, a Delhi Township native, graduated from Seton High School, Price Hill, and the College of Mount St. Joseph, Delhi. S. Barbara is the first graduate of Seton High School to ever be elected head of the congregation. She is also the first native Cincinnatian to hold the highest office in more than 30 years.

S. Barbara has served on the executive council for the past eight years and been in charge of such congregational projects as Gathering 1998 and the renovation of the Immaculate Conception Chapel, completed in 2000 She will remain on the current renovation committee for the Motherhouse and is the creator of the slogan,

"Renovation is our friend." S. Barbara also served as executive treasurer, so employees saw her name on their paychecks.

S. Barbara has served as a high school English teacher; the congregation's director of formation; administrator of Julie Penrose Center, a retreat center in Colorado Springs, Colo.; and vice president of mission effectiveness at Penrose-St. Francis Health Care System, Colorado Springs.

S. Barbara's office and all the executive offices are located in the east wing of the college. Her assistant is Kathi Zeinner.

S. Barbara Hagedorn's reflection during the July 6 ceremony focused on the theme of light, which was introduced in the procession when S. Mary Ellen Murphy carried in a wide-rimmed bowl holding a candle "to remind us of how we are walking into our future--as women of faith guided by God's light," S. Barbara explained.

"Elizabeth Seton knew that seeking the light was essential for the spiritual journey. She encourages us to keep seeking the direction for our future with these words: 'I will cling and hold to my God...begging for that light and never change until I find it.' Following the course set before us, we come with gratitude and expectation, looking to God to be our light in a fragile world. We are challenged and called to be signs of hope, called to be people of integrity--watching, waiting and living in the light," said S. Barbara.

S. Nancy Bramlage, councilor

S. Nancy Bramlage has been living in New York City where she was an associate in the Sisters of Charity Federation non-governmental organization (NGO) office. Prior to that position S. Nancy served as director of the Center for Social Concern at the University of Dayton, Dayton, Ohio, her hometown.

S. Nancy has been a French teacher and a missionary in Malawi, Africa. She has also served as congregational liaison to the foreign missions and personnel director, and has served on many boards and advisory committees.

As councilor S. Nancy will oversee ministry, full-time study and renewal of the Sisters, working with S. Patricia Mary Malarkey. She will also spearhead <u>social</u>
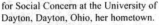
/ justice activities, including serving as the Congregation's NGO representative to the Sisters of Charity Federation.

S. Nancy's assistant is Tina Mersmann.

Sister Rita Celine sponsored Sister Nancy for the Sisters of Charity of Cincinnati.

S. Mary Michele Fischer, councilor *"Marieh"*

S. Mary Michele Fischer, a Detroit, Mich., native, has served in the West for the past 25 years. She taught in elementary, secondary and adult education in Michigan, Ohio, Maryland and Colorado; was program director at the Julie Penrose Center in Colorado Springs; and was coordinator of Pace e Bene Nonviolence Center in Las Vegas, Nev. She also served in leadership roles among the Sisters of Charity of Cincinnati in the Western Network.

S. Mary Michele will work with the Spirituality Center, the Associate program, and Sisters considering or enjoying retirement.

S. Mary Michele's assistant will be Jan Harvey.

S. Maureen Heverin, councilor

S. Maureen Heverin, a Cincinnati native, has served on the executive council since 1999. S. Maureen was on the Gathering 2002/Chapter 2003 planning committee and is the congregation's representative on the Sisters of Charity Federation Executive Committee.

Sister will also assume the oversight of women going through the formation process, working with the Vocation Team and with S. Mary Kay Bush. As liaison to the Central Network she will be working with many of the Sisters in the Motherhouse and Mother Margaret Hall.

Prior to serving on council S. Maureen served as case manager at Welcome House in Covington, Ky., and as formation director for the congregation. Originally a teacher at elementary schools in Maryland, and Xenia and Cincinnati, Ohio, she taught teens and adults working on basic literacy and preparing for their GED at HUB and Terrace Guild in Cincinnati.

S. Maureen's assistant is Tina Mersmann.

S. Georgia Kitt, councilor

S. Georgia Kitt was born and raised in Carroll, Iowa. For the last 10 years she has been director of the guidance department and director of admissions at Bishop Fenwick High School, the largest high school in the Archdiocese of Boston, Mass. Prior to that Sister Georgia served as counselor, math teacher, assistant principal and principal in high schools in Springfield and Chillicothe, Ohio. She was also a member of the congregation's Eastern Network Leadership for nine years.

As councilor Sister will oversee Communications and the Motherhouse campus. She has also been named executive treasurer, meaning S. Georgia's name will now appear on the paychecks. Sisters Georgia and Joan Patrice Flynn are now renting a house on Charity Drive in Bridgetown. How appropriate!

S. Georgia's assistant is Jan Harvey.

I met with Barbara Hagedorn, SC in 2003 and the sexual abuse policy was revied in 2003. Could be a coincidence!

SEXUAL ABUSE POLICY

Sisters of Charity of Cincinnati

Original 1995
Revised 2003

SEXUAL ABUSE POLICY
PHILOSOPHY and GUIDING PRINCIPLES

The Sisters of Charity of Cincinnati are committed to providing a communal and ministerial environment that gives, nourishes and defends life.

> *"Through our ministries we seek to transform the world*
> *into a more just one and to uncover and nurture what*
> *is good and beautiful in the world."*
>
> (SC Constitutions 6, p. 8)

The Congregation takes seriously any allegations of sexual abuse against minors[1] and vulnerable adults[2] by its members and responds immediately in a pastoral, compassionate and responsible manner. With the ultimate aim of reconciling and bringing healing, the Congregation pledges to treat justly, respectfully and compassionately everyone involved in such cases.

Within the context of this document the term "abuse" is intended to refer to sexual abuse of minors and vulnerable adults. The documents of the Congregation form the basis and framework for the implementation of this policy for its members.

All members of the Congregation must do all in their power to prevent such behavior. All members are expected to educate themselves on

---

[1] A minor is any person under the age of 18.
[2] Vulnerable adults are persons as defined in applicable state statutes.

this issue, and they are expected to be aware of and abide by this policy

Any accusation will be taken seriously and the investigation and resolution will be driven by pastoral concern for all involved. The President and Council will incorporate the following guiding principles in responding to such allegations.

▶ LISTENING

The act of listening will be done with sensitivity, respect and compassion and without judgment or prejudice:
- to any person who presents an allegation that he or she has been harmed by a member of the Congregation;
- to the member who is the subject of the allegation.

▶ RESPONSIBILITIES

In undertaking any action the President and Council will bear in mind the need to balance the right of every individual to protection from sexual abuse, on the one hand, and the right of a potentially innocent person to preservation of her good name, on the other. To this end the President and Council will proceed responsibly in

2.

keeping with justice toward the person who was allegedly abused
- with sufficient scrutiny to determine if there seems to be reliable evidence of misconduct;
- by informing the member that her behavior is the subject of an allegation of abuse.

Each member of the Congregation has the responsibility to inform the President of the Congregation of any reasonably suspected, sexually abusive behavior with minors or vulnerable adults on the part of any member, even in the absence of an accusation by a reported victim.

Any member who is accused of such behavior needs to immediately inform the President or her Network Leader If the Network Leader is the first to be informed she will immediately contact the President. The member is not to discuss any aspect of the allegation with other persons.

▶ CONFIDENTIALITY

All persons enjoy the right of privacy and the right to a good name. The President and Council will therefore:
- proceed appropriately in the investigation so as to safeguard the privacy and good name of the person who has made the allegation, and of the member who is the subject of the allegation;

3.

- will comply with the required legal reporting statutes and will inform the victim of this, as well as the accused member

▶ **FOLLOW-UP**

- The President and Council will manifest pastoral care for the victim as well as the family in the case of a minor
- Out of pastoral concern, the President and Council may, in appropriate circumstances, offer the alleged victim or victims, (including immediate families in the case of a minor) support and financial assistance to obtain professional counseling while a formal investigation of the allegation is taking place. This action will be in consultation with legal counsel and the congregation's insurance carrier
- The President and Council will manifest pastoral care for the member accused.
- The President and Council will manifest pastoral care for all other members who also suffer when they learn that a member has been accused of sexual abuse.
- The President will share appropriate information with Congregational members.
- The President will offer assistance for understanding and healing within the Congregation in this difficult and sensitive situation.

4.

▶ **PUBLIC RELATIONS AND MEDIA**

- Only the President of the Sisters of Charity and/or her specified delegate will respond to all public and media inquiries.
- This communication will be done in a manner consistent with the demands of confidentiality

END NOTES

■ This policy may be used as appropriate for cases of sexual misconduct with adults.

■ This policy applies to members of the Congregation and may serve as a guideline as appropriate in cases involving former members while they were members of the Congregation.

■ This policy has been approved by Executive Council of the Sisters of Charity on March 10, 2003.

5.

Sisters of Charity
of Cincinnati

Thank you
- you I CON you

CONFIDENTIAL

FOR SISTERS ONLY

February 10, 2006

Dear Sister,

This new year brings with it a serious matter which I feel is important to share with you. It is with a heavy heart that I write this letter. I regret to inform you that an allegation of sexual abuse of a minor by a Sister of Charity has been made. After consultation, I have engaged an independent investigator to carry out an investigation of the allegation in order to help determine the facts. The investigator may find it necessary to contact a few members of the Congregation. If you are contacted I hope that you will cooperate and provide the information requested.

I ask that you keep this information confidential. Please do not share it with anyone who is not a Sister of Charity. This is extremely important. While the investigation is going on, it is important that nothing about the allegation be discussed. Keep in mind that this is an allegation at this point. After the investigation has been completed, I will be in contact with you about this matter. This may take some time.

As a Congregation we once again renew our commitment to protect minors and vulnerable adults. Let us hold in prayer those who are part of this allegation and hold each other in prayer.

May God's spirit be with us all.

Your sister,

Barbara

Barbara Hagedorn, SC
President

(After reading this letter, please shred it. Thank you.)

Office of the President

Letter to the Sisters of Charity of Cincinnati from President Barbara Hagedorn, SC regarding an allegation of sexual abuse against one of the Sisters. The leaf is from my friend's grave.

7-24-04

We are the Sisters of Charity.
But first, we are
human beings. We be-
gan with a very human saint,
Elizabeth, and branched out
with a stalwart Margaret.

Our history is pretty well
known to us. We have our
heroines and our we have
those we remember with
painful feelings.

As our Community grew
numerous, the structure
became unwieldly. Rule
upon rule — the eye on
the speck, the rigid con-
trol, the tightening of the
screws, the power with the
few — we strained out the
gnats and swallowed the
camels.

Yet, the Holy Spirit hung on,
for some of us are still here
after an explosion that blew
the lids off. We lost some
of our finest. We shrunk.
We repented and put our
heads together and began

Copy of a handwrtten letter of support to Sisters of Charity of Cincinnati President Barbara Hagdoen, SC from Mary Jo Jay, SC. A transcription of the letter is printed on page 139.

2

The weather today: _____

to renew ourselves and

A Prayer Journal

Today I feel: our ways.

We continue to grow each
day and try to actually own

Today I am grateful for our title of Charity.
We pray, we act, we serve,
we suffer. We tackle the
hard things, we try.

Inspirations, prayer, scriptures, notes: St. Paul warned
His Christians that Evil would
be jealous and would renew
his efforts to freeze our.

I said a special prayer for: Charity.
How often we say, "I am
for the underdog." But, is

Prayer(s) answered (comfort, peace, love and miracles): it true?
There are still among us those
who would control the "undesirable" elements of human

Donations of the Heart (acts of kindness, sharing, caring, and forgiveness) _____
behavior. Just sweep them all
under the rug. Don't talk
about it; you'll disturb someone.

What I would like to see happen tomorrow (Goals, ideas, etc.): _____
I, myself, am no one in par-
ticular. Being quite vulnerable,
I listen to those who
have no "clout."

"Coincidence is God's way of remaining anonymous"

© 1999 Journals Unlimited, Inc., Bay City, MI The *"Write It Down"* Series

There are a couple of friends of mine who have been treated quite shoddily, dismissed with cold finality for daring to be "different". Their issues are pertinent and should be respectfully heard. ~~and acted upon~~

But, then, things might be embarrassing or even ~~scandalous~~ if brought out of the closet where they dwell with skeletons we even joke about now.

Maybe something can be done to make amends. Maybe an apology? Maybe a little soul searching? We are all accountable.

Let us pray and offer any suffering that a day may bring, to redeem ourselves and truly be Sisters of Charity.

Call me if you don't understand or want specifics. 451-8253

Transcription of handwritten note above from Mary Jo Jay, SC.

July 29, 2004

Dear Barbara,

We are the Sisters of Charity. But first we are human beings. We began with a very human saint, Elizabeth, and branched out with a stalwart Margaret.

Our history is pretty well known to us. We have our heroines and we have those we remember with painful feelings.

As our community grew numerous, the structure became unwieldly. Rule upon rule – the eye on the speck, the rigid control, the tightening of the screws, the power of the few. We strained out the gnats and swallowed the camels.

Yet the Holy Spirit hung on, for some of us are still here after an explosion that blew the lids off. We lost some of our finest, we shrunk. We repented and put our heads together and began to renew ourselves and our ways.

We continue to grow each day and try to actually own our title of Charity. We pray, we act, we serve, we suffer, we tackle the hard things, we try.

St. Paul warned His Christians that Evil would be jealous and would renew his efforts to freeze our charity.

How often we say, "I am for the Underdog." But is it true? There are still among us those who would control the undesirable elements of human behavior. Just sweep them all under the rug. Don't talk about it; you'll disturb someone.

I, myself, am no one in particular. Being quite vulnerable, I listen to those who have no "clout'.

There are a couple of friends of mine who have been treated quite shoddily, dismissed with cold finality for daring to be "different'. Their issues are pertinent and should be respectfully heard. But things might be embarrassing or even scandalous if brought out of the closet where they dwell with skeletons we even joke about now.

Maybe something can be done to make amends. Maybe an apology? Maybe a little soul searching? We are all accountable.

Let us pray and offer any suffering that a day now brings, to redeem ourselves and truly be Sisters of Charity.

(Call me if you don't understand or want specifics.)

Sister Mary Jo left her phone number.

My mother and Mary Jo Jay, SC, at my Bayley Place home owned and operated by the Sisters of Charity of Cincinnati.

MJJ's Psalm 151

STOP FIGHTING, MARY
YOU'RE PERMANENTLY MARGINALIZED
YOU HAVE A MENTAL ILLNESS.
TO MANY, YOU ARE NO LONGER CREDIBLE.

BUT TO YOU, O GOD, I CAN SHARE
   WHAT IS UNIQUE IN ALL THE WORLD·

      the ecstacy of mania
      the agony of depression
      the try at oblivion
      the resurrection
      the healing
      the revelation that I am loved divinely.

TO CHRIST'S SUFFERINGS, I OFFER.

      the locked solitary room
      the being tied, spread-eagled, to a bed
      the shock treatments
      the demoralization
      the observation window
      the ton of medication
      the side effect of purple skin
      the warinessof people who "know"
      the life long burden of one who is marked.

AND, TO YOU, O FATHER, I REJOICE.

      in the euphoric dancing
      at the burst of creativity
      with the company of the afflicted
      of the warmth of those who don't give a damn.

ALSO, I SEEM TO BE SOMEWHAT EMPTIED TO RECEIVE THE
HOLY SPIRIT IN HER FIRE AND TRUTH, THE PANORAMA OF
GOD'S LOVE ENHANCES EACH NEW DAY

Sister Mary Jo Jay's 151st Psalm. (Note: There are only 150 Psalms in the Bible.)
Mary Jo is describing part of her life.

August 11, 2005

Dear Barbara,

It has been more than a year since I made an appointment to meet with you to talk about how we as community are going to respond to Linda Mahlmeister's need. It was a hard meeting for me and it took me about nine months too get the courage up to ask to talk with you. This was not because you are unapproachable but because of the nature of the issues needing discussion.

In my annual retreat prior to requesting the meeting last summer I processed my own felt sense or complicity. Later in personal prayer at home I experienced a profound sense of grief- an agony in the garden- that took me to my knees sobbing. That gift of prayerful release empowered me to write a poem which I later read to the whole council at our meeting some months later. This was when the council met with my ministry support group and we talked for the first time about how the community needs to pastorally respond to Linda and to one another around these abuse issues.

Barb, this whole process has become an ordeal that is taking a toll on my health. The long lapses between meetings that give us opportunity to look at our obligation to Linda are painful to me. I don't know how it has been for you, similar I suppose. We need to take action on Linda's behalf and this needs to be sooner rather than later. And it needs to be action in direct response to what she has disclosed and requested.

I want to see us give her a formal letter of remorse for what she experienced at the hand of Rita Celine. This letter would express heart felt sorrow and contrition for emotional, spiritual, physical, social pain she has experienced for 47 years now. It would also let her know that the expense she incurred for therapy can be reimbursed to her. It would thank her for being a part of Bayley Village and re-invite her to continue living there should she wish or offer to talk with her about terms of release from the financial agreement she signed while under the impression she was personally invited by you, Barb. [If I were you I'd arrange with the financial executive and/or attorney for a release of that lease/ purchase agreement with offer to refund the money Linda has bound in that agreement if she request a release.]

The letter should tell her that the retreat she requested is being addressed by a group of sisters who are planning a way for the Sisters and Associates to address the need for recovery and healing from the oppressions and abuses the system of religious life has perpetrated. The letter should thank Linda for her courage and her compassion toward us in trying to get a response that is justified. It should thank her for being faithful to her struggle and for being an example of Charity in adversity.

Personally, I believe Linda has been a martyr in the religious sense for our communal sins. I feel such a need for a communal forum of repentance for this social sin for which we all bear culpability by virtue of our bonds of community.

Letter of support from Dee Sizler, SC to President Barbara Hagedorn, SC.

I really need your support, Barb, first, sister-to-sister and then as our discerned leader. You have the grace and authority to do a wonderful caring, healing act of Charity and I call you to this.

Actually this whole affair is an invitation to grace and renewal by our God who suffered for us and wants only for us to relinquish our bonds of oppression. We are so blessed, aren't we? These dark emotional experiences are none the less holy than our celebrations of joy We can embrace this opportunity to love as we are loved. I anticipate such joy in our facing this boldly and with the confidence of those who are committed to the urging charity of Christ.

Thank you, Barbara, and I eagerly await your response, a phone call will due.

Blessings and love,

Dee Sizler, SC and Lucy at my home at Bayley Place in Cincinnati.

August 10, 2005

Dear Barb;

I am writing to you regarding a concern I have about the Community and the manner in which it is handling issues of sexual/physical abuse by members of our Congregation.

It has come to my attention that there is an accusation from a former member and present Associate member of the congregation. I don't know the particulars of the accusation, nor do I care too. But the information I have been given is that the Sisters of Charity community has done nothing, not even offered to pay for counseling, for this individual even though we have known of the accusations for a couple of years.

As a victim of abuse, my biggest fear about telling was that no one would believe me. Thank God, when I finally was brave enough to say something, I was not ignored or labeled as a liar

As you know, the news as of late about the Roman Catholic Church and their handling of the abuse issue has turned into scandal because of how the Church dealt with or rather didn't deal with the accusations. I am saddened that my church chose to be more concerned about their reputation, and the legal and monetary ramifications than the victims. I find myself ashamed of my church and am appalled that the leadership (I use that term loosely) of the Archdiocese of Cincinnati continues to show their lack of concern for the true victims in this whole mess even today after ample time to educate themselves about the issue of abuse and those who commit this crime.

I beg you, as a past victim and as a member of the congregation of the Sisters of Charity of Cincinnati, to start to openly and honestly deal with this victim and any other victims that may have come forward. Choose to worry about the victims and not our reputation and legal/monetary security. In the name of justice please don't do what our church has done to its membership.

Thank you for taking time to attend to my concern.

cc: Linda Mahlmeister

Letter of support to President Barbara Hagedorn, SC.

February 21, 2006

Sister Barbara Hagedorn SC,
Executive Offices
5900 Delhi Rd.
Mt. St. Joseph, Ohio 45051

Dear Barb,

I am writing to you because for several months now I have sat back and watched a dear friend of mine, Linda Mahlmeister, suffer at the hands of my own Sisters. Even though she has left the state, she continues to suffer due to your silence.

From the time she came to you wanting to work with our community to proactively address the sexual abuse done to her by Rita Celine, she has been discarded and shunned. I cannot tell you how much this saddens me. That we can treat another human being with such blatant indifference and then collectively condone such behavior is unfathomable to me as a Sister of Charity. How is this justifiable in anyone's heart? Or mind?

For the record, I believe Linda was sexually abused by Rita Celine. I believe that we as a community are responsible for what Rita Celine's behavior dictated. Clearly, Rita was a disturbed individual. Either we bear out that responsibility or we become complicit with Rita's denial. There is no gray area in this, Barb.

I know it is hard for our own Sisters to comprehend how sexual abuse affects someone. It is not something one can get "over." I am asking you, Barb, to open your heart to a new compassion for Linda. She deserves to be set free. We can help her. I cannot understand why, at the very least, we don't offer her compensation for her therapy. My God, she is 62

Letter of support from Diana Bode, SC to President Barbara Hagedorn, SC.

years of age. Doing that would help her.

Talking to people from The Voice of the Faithful and in reading their articles, those who have been sexually abused by priests and/or religious are forced to sue as the last resort because the perpetrator refuses to take responsibility for the abuse.

Linda's "truth" will not go away, but will rise again and again in the name of justice. We as a community can face this challenge and grow stronger for having made the journey. I firmly believe that we, as women religious, have an opportunity and an obligation to serve our Church by developing and engaging with other religious communities to provide a healing strategy in a loving and nurturing way, for those who have suffered sexual abuse by priests and/or religious.

I would appreciate a response.

Prayerfully,

Diana Bode, SC

Diana Bode, S.C.

Me and Diana Bode, SC in Aruba.

Linda Mahlmeister

$CO\!f\!(\!$

September 2, 2006

Barbara Hagedorn, SC
President of Sisters of Charity of Cincinnati
5900 Delhi Rd.
Mount St. Joseph, OH 45051

Dear Barb·

This letter is an overdue response to your request that I contact you, which I appreciate.
Diana shared your letter of March of this year with me, and I have purposely taken time
to try to get to a more peaceful place, regarding my history with the Sisters of Charity

You will recall from my letter to you and to the Executive Council in 2004, I felt that
when I finally found the courage to meet with you regarding my sexual abuse by Rita
Celine Weadick, SC, you did not respond as I had hoped. After our second meeting, I left
feeling stunned and rejected. I am not saying that was your intent, but that is how I felt. I
had come with the hope of finding a way to continue my healing within the Community,
and left feeling unwanted. I had also requested to meet with you and the Executive
Council and was not given that courtesy

As time passed, I found it too painful to continue to live at Bayley Place. The view from
my window overlooked your Executive offices, and I began having "custody of the eyes"
just to cope. Also I endured shunning, as if I were an outcast, from Sisters, some on the
Executive Council. I experienced this as a complete disregard for me as a human being. I
realized this was not how I wanted to live and made the financially and emotionally
painful decision to leave my beautiful home and my dreams of a spiritual life of service
with the Sisters on the Mother House grounds, which remain holy grounds for me.

I have used the time since moving to Florida to continue my healing and also to try to
understand your position and the lack of response from any member of the Executive
Council. I confronted you with something out of the blue, not of your making, and asked
you to respond to what I thought would be a healing process. I have heard from members
of the Community that you and the Executive Council simply did not know what to do. I
have also heard that some felt that I was "crazy or needed help." Barb, I am now more
able to understand this. I can imagine that it was disturbing to have to face something that
did not fit the image of a Sister of Charity of Cincinnati, to see the pain it had caused, and
to be afraid of possible legal action or public exposure. I can also understand how much
you may have wanted to deny what you were hearing and might even pray that it would
all go away I have been doing that since I was fifteen years old, but we both know that
feelings and facts do not just go away

What can we do to move beyond where we are? I believe the Community could demonstrate both caring and some accountability for my sexual abuse by compensating me for part of my financial losses incurred from this entire experience. I lost over $42,000 by breaking my contract with Bayley Place, a contract I would have never broken were I not desperate. As I have previously stated, my expenses for past therapy exceeded $60,000 Compensating me for Bailey Place would cost the Community very little, if any, as you have made money on the resale of my unit. But it would mean a great deal to me especially at the age of sixty-two on a fixed income. Financial compensation is a standard practice in our culture when a wrong has been committed, and it would assist me in letting go and moving on. Also, I still believe that you, the Executive Council, and the entire Community would benefit by opening your hearts and having an open ongoing discussion of the pain within the Community around sexual abuse issues. As you and I are both aware, there are even some Sisters of Charity who have been sexually abused, and in some cases the perpetrators are/have been members of the Community Sadly, no Pope, to date, has set a good example, but you could chart a new course.

What can I do? In various ways, I can continue to work everyday to take responsibility for my own life and try to reach a place of wholeness and forgiveness. It took me at least thirty-three years to separate Rita from the rest of the Community, and now I am struggling again to deal with the trauma of how I have been treated since I decided to disclose my sexual abuse to you and members of the Community I have long ago accepted that what happened to me at fifteen changed who I am, but I believe that it had purpose. Although my life has not unfolded as I wanted, I have faith that I am being guided on my spiritual journey Presently, I see no reason to re-contact SNAP or Voice of the Faithful. My experience from attending their meetings is that they do not wish to focus on religious sisters or nuns as sexual perpretators. They seem to feel more comfortable admitting and dealing with priests as sexual perpetrators, but like many, they seem to be in denial of such unimaginable behavior from the female gender We need to look at not the shadow side, not the dark, but the black, evil side of women religious.

These are my suggestions for finding a path to healing to which you referred, and I would be open to hearing your ideas. If you still have doubts about the truth of what happened to me, I would suggest that you speak with Elizabeth Cashman, SC and Joan Groff, SC. As you are aware dialog is essential to reaching an accord regarding any matter and that dialog must be governed by respect so that all are free to express their views. Therefore, I would appreciate your response to me at the above address.

Thank you for your time and consideration.

Sincerely,

Linda Mahlmeister

Letter I sent to President Barbara Hagedorn, SC requesting financial compensation for my sexual abuse. Now that I'm talking about money, I hear from her that she will set up an investigation interview.

Sisters of Charity
of Cincinnati

November 13, 2006

Linda Mahlmeister

Dear Linda,

Thank you for your letter dated September 2. Like you I wanted to take some time to reflect on your response before I replied. I appreciate your getting in touch with me again.

I have shared your letter with the Council. Before making a decision we want to talk to several people as you have suggested. I also wanted to let you know that several religious congregations have formed a Review Board of professionals from various disciplines to review allegations that are made. The Board can offer valuable insights. Because it is an objective board it is most helpful for all involved.

In the next few months I will have someone contact you and others who might have recollections regarding the allegations. Also you will be asked for names of people you want to be contacted to provide information. After the contacts have been made, a written report will be given to the Review Board for their consideration. The Board will then submit its findings to me and the Council for our decision.

Then I will be in touch with you to let you know our response. The process may take some time so I ask for your patience as we proceed.

I continue to pray for you and ask God's grace and healing.

Sincerely,

Barbara

Barbara Hagedorn, SC

Office of the President
5900 Delhi Road
Mount St. Joseph, Ohio 45051
(513) 347-5200 • FAX: (513) 347-5228
www.srcharitycinti.org

Letter from President Barbara Hagedorn, SC informing me of a Review Board to look into allegations of alleged sexual abuse.

Sisters of Charity
of Cincinnati

February 1, 2007

Linda Mahlmeister

Dear Linda,

Greetings from Ohio where winter has finally arrived. I hope you are doing well.

I am writing to let you know that Sister Pat, a Dominican sister, will be in touch with you to set up a time to meet. However I realized I do not have your phone number to give her If you could send it to me, I will pass it on right away The two of you can then make the necessary arrangements for your meeting.

Thanks, Linda.

Sincerely,

Barbara

Barbara Hagedorn, SC

Office of the President
5900 Delhi Road
Mount St. Joseph, Ohio 45051
(513) 347-5200 • FAX: (513) 347-5228
www.srcharitycinti.org

Letter from President Barbara Hagedorn, SC informing me that a Dominican Sister Pat will be interviewing me, which was the decision of the Review Board.

Sisters of Charity
of Cincinnati

October 11, 2007

Linda Mahlmeister

Dear Linda,

I wanted to give you an update on the progress of the investigation. Sister Patricia Twohill has completed her report. At this time the chair of the Review Board is calling a meeting of the board to review the report and make recommendations. This should happen in the next few months. After they submit their recommendations to the Council per our policy, I will be in touch with you.

Not long ago I heard that your mother died. I would like to extend my sympathy and prayers to you. May she rest in peace.

Sincerely,

Barbara Hagedorn, SC

Barbara Hagedorn, SC

> *Letter from President Barbara Hagedorn, SC informing me that Sister Pat had completed her investigation and that the Review Board will make their decision and submit it to the Executive Council.*

Office of the President
5900 Delhi Road
Mount St. Joseph, Ohio 45051
(513) 347-5200 • FAX: (513) 347-5228
www.srcharitycinti.org

Sisters of Charity
of Cincinnati

January 12, 2008

Linda Mahlmeister

Dear Linda:

Thank you for your patience and cooperation during the time that the Sisters of Charity have authorized an independent investigation to address your allegation of sexual abuse by Sister Rita Celine. We are sorry for the pain you have experienced through all of this.

The investigator, Sister Pat (who is not affiliated with the Sisters of Charity), was able to interview persons identified by both you and the Sisters of Charity who might provide pertinent information at the time period of the allegation. The entire report from the investigator was presented to an objective Review Board. A recommendation from the Review Board was given to me and the Executive Council of the Sisters of Charity for our decision.

The Council and I have carefully considered the board's recommendation and have reached our decision based on their recommendation. The investigation was unable to prove or disprove the allegations of sexual abuse by Sister Rita Celine alleged to have taken place between the years of 1960-1965. In part, this is because Sister Rita Celine, who died in 1996, had no opportunity to respond to your allegation. No other allegations have been made against her. We have taken your concerns seriously and have followed our policies in responding to this allegation.

Out of pastoral concern for you in your healing process, the Sisters of Charity would offer to pay for six months of counseling or 25 sessions with a licensed therapist/counselor. If further counseling is requested the therapist will be asked to give an evaluation of the first six months and make a recommendation for up to an additional six months of counseling. Please let me know if you wish to pursue the counseling so that we can arrange method of payment.

I realize this period of waiting for a response has been a difficult one. Be assured of my continued prayers and those of the Sisters of Charity.

Sincerely,

Barbara Hagedorn, SC

Sister Barbara Hagedorn, SC

Office of the President
5900 Delhi Road
Mount St. Joseph, Ohio 45051
(513) 347-5200 • FAX: (513) 347-5228
www.srcharitycinti.org

Certified letter from President Barbara Hagedorn, SC informing me that the investigation was unable to prove or disprive the allegations of sexual abuse by Sister Rita Celine ,and offered me a low ball token of 25 counselling sessions. I did not respond.

Above: My home at The Village of Bayley Place. The back of my home looked over at the offices of the Executive Council of the Sisters of Charity at Cincinnati.

Left: Mom's 87th birthday at home in Bayley Place.

Right: (Left to Right) Me with Joan Groff, SC, and Elizabeth Cashman, SC (AKA John Christopher, SC), at my home in Bayley Place.

Tuesday, June 27, 2005

Dear Joan,

Again thank you for your welcomed call and interest/effort on behalf of all who have been sexually abused by Sister/Nuns.

Enclosed are copies of the letters I discussed with you on June 18. Please feel free to share them with your group

You are in my daily prayer life

Linda

239-731-1035

Letter of appreciation to Joan Groff, SC

"I LOVE PEOPLE WHO HARNESS THEMSELVES, AN OX TO A HEAVY CART, WHO PULL LIKE WATER BUFFALO, WITH MASSIVE PATIENCE, WHO STRAIN IN THE MUD AND THE MUCK TO MOVE THINGS FORWARD, WHO DO WHAT HAS TO BE DONE, AGAIN AND AGAIN."

— MARGE PIERCY

CHAPTER EIGHT

THE TRUE GENESIS OF MY STORY

Over the years, I've been puzzled over why I was so vulnerable to the abusive relationship with Sister Rita Celine. I have worn the dark cloak of shame, embarrassment, and guilt that all victims of sexual abuse wear. I ask myself how could I have been so naïve, and why couldn't I put on the brakes long before I found the wisdom and strength to slam them on?

I even ask, why did she choose me? This is perhaps the most haunting question for victims, because implied in the asking is the possibility of our own personal responsibility—what did I do or say to invite this?

In my own case, I have also wondered, at times, if I had been straight, (heterosexual), would I have permitted such behavior to occur? I will never know this answer for sure because I was not conscious or ready to admit to myself that I was a lesbian until I was thirty-seven. If I had been sexually educated in the home, church, or school, including the existence of homosexuality, I would have known who I was and what we were doing together.

Sister Rita Celine's behavior, as with any other perpetrator, is about exerting power over her victim. I now know that my sexual identity did not make any difference.

Now, when I look back, it is quite easy to see Sister Rita Celine's pattern of behavior and the steps of my submission. She was a classic, repeat predator who saw my vulnerability and innocence and took advantage of it. The why of my vulnerability is more essential to me for my peace of mind, and for that I turn to my background for the answers.

My Dad grew up on a farm in rural Ohio, as did Sister Rita Celine Weadick. These families had shared values—independence, hard work, simplicity.

Thus, in one sense, Sister Rita Celine "knew" who I was because of shared backgrounds. My mother's father was a factory worker, her mother a homemaker. Dayton, Ohio in the 1940-1950's was a small place, far from sophisticated city life or urban culture.

People who escaped the dreariness of farming, as some of these people did, were glad to shake the dust off their feet, but the journey from homestead to Dayton's streets was a short one. As I grew up, visits to my paternal grandparents continued, with their values and fresh produce streaming toward and converging in our home.

My family appeared to be "ordinary" Americans—midwestern, religious, the salt of the earth. My Dad came to town because his parents told him that he would fail at farming; my Mother came to the relationship, leaving behind a burdensome mother who, in the deepest sense, never "let her go".

As so often happens, my parents played out the roles handed to them by their families. Dad was the firstborn in 1908 and had two younger brothers; his background was German-English, and the religious influence was Quaker, Amish and Brethren.

The family claimed its American origins could be traced to

Captain John Smith and Pocahontas. (I have never checked out this family anecdote.) Leaving the farm after high school graduation, Dad continued what he had enjoyed there: playing the clarinet, maintaining engines, and "tinkering" with anything mechanical. It relaxed him.

I can still picture his head under the hood of his car, grease up to his elbows, in his bib overhauls, carefully disassembling the engine and making it whole again. When my parents married, Dad converted to Catholicism.

Dayton was then a factory town. Dad took a job with National Cash Register (NCR) and was company trained as a mechanical engineer. He worked there for 32 years and handed his paycheck over to Mom. Dad retired when NCR downsized and changed from mechanical to electronic operation.

Dad had a goofy, splendid sense of humor, was affectionate and responsible. I inherited his laughter, love of animals and trees, and his respect for wooden furniture where he could see life in the transformed wood. He taught me to be respectful and to keep my word. Surely, in our family, his favorite was my older sister, Carol, who found great comfort in his love, which always delighted me.

When he moved to Dayton, he was introduced to Mom. She was six years younger, a Roman Catholic of German-French decent, and also the eldest, with five younger siblings. Her mother had married at age sixteen, had three children in succession, then had a nervous breakdown and handed family responsibility over to my Mom.

Being the eldest, my Mom had to buy and prepare food, wash clothes, clean house, and control her younger siblings. When one has to control, one tends to be controlling.

My Mom and Grandmother had a friendship or cohort relationship, rather than mother-daughter relationship. They seemed to be in charge of their family. Like her mother, my mother never drove a car (or wore slacks), so we would ride the bus to our grandparents' home where the two of them would discuss the family. Mom was like a counselor to Grandmother.

Grandmother would chew (that's what my family called it when one talks about an issue over and over and over) about one of her children until finally my Mom would say, "Mom, shut up about it." Then Dad would pick us up in our car and we would go home.

Although they continued their family bond for sixty-some years, my mother eventually severed all ties with her family when she disagreed with some of their decisions. But by the time my Grandmother died in 1989, their ambivalent relationship had permanently erased whatever possibilities may have existed for my Mother to be free of anger and fear which caused her to need to dominate.

As the nine-year-old mini-housewife, who ran the home, my Mom, had been cheated out of her childhood. On her deathbed, she was still reliving the unfairness of this. From that early injustice, she developed a keen sense of how to control others and demand total obedience.

Any good memories of her childhood she had were comprised of tiny facets of the picture; roller skating to her aunt's and grandparents' home with messages for them—before the age of telephones—or winning praise from her Dad for her expertise in the kitchen. The way to people's hearts and wills, she may have reasoned, was through their stomachs.

When I was growing up, holidays meant a frenzy of cooperative baking, much of it with fruit from our grandparents' farm and our backyard garden. The cherries, pears, plums, peaches, apples, and apricots from our 32 fruit trees went into cookies and pies; we canned grape juice, as well as most of our vegetables.

I remember a local restaurant owner talking with my parents about paying Mom for her delicious pies and cinnamon pecan rolls. I doubt she ever did sell her baking as she was busy enough in her daily life. I also remember her delight when she did not bake for about two years, while I worked at Belmont Bakery (which was next to Immaculate Conception Church).

On Saturday evenings, we would box up left over baked goods. The owner donated these items to St. Joseph Orphanage. He also let us take some home. My Dad always picked me up after work. My family enjoyed Boston cream pie, whipped cream pies of all kinds, cakes, cookies, and donuts. My Mom was so happy to receive these baked sweets.

Christmas was a "big deal" at our home, and in addition to baking and cooking, it also featured alcohol at family parties. My Dad's people forbade alcohol on their premises, but my maternal grandparents had beer at every party, and no one ever misbehaved. Their brown bottled beer and pop was iced down in a gray washtub.

At our house, the end of harvest and Christmas led to family celebrations—Dad went to the neighborhood tavern with a jug which had a small round glass handle and got it half filled with draft beer, foam on top. We all sat around the kitchen table while Mom brought out pimento cheese glasses and pretzels and yellow mustard. As soon as Dad got back, beverages were served. One year we kids asked for a taste of the beer. My parents conferred, and Dad poured a fourth of the glass, to where the flowered border was printed on the glass. Each of us tasted the bitter brew, and then we asked for a Coke.

My Dad never drank more than two alcoholic drinks at a time because it gave him hiccups, and during her whole life, Mom probably never finished a six-pack a year. However, I acquired a taste for it as a teenager trying to handle Sister Rita Celine's advances. It was an inadequate and dangerous coping method.

During my life, I have experienced dark periods when I have abused alcohol. This self-medication was a direct consequence of being sexually abused, my attempt to drown the pain, confusion and depression.

My mother's family belonged to St. Mary's Parish in Dayton, Ohio—I mean literally belonged to the church. Great grandmother, and then grandmother, ironed the linens and supported the Holy Rosary society.

We always prayed the Rosary and said grace before meals, cooked for festivals, prayed at church for special intentions, and attended Mass daily. Even the next generation was whipped into form by performing musically in the Church choir and Catholic school orchestra. Mom played the piano, her sister the violin. Years later, I wanted to learn to play the piano, and mother said, "No". Perhaps the thought brought up unpleasant memories of being forced to perform. At the age of 12, my mother almost drowned because she didn't know how to swim. Therefore, she made sure that her children knew how to swim.

From Mom, I learned to love animals, entertaining, cooking and respect for money. Carol said I could make a buffalo squeal off a nickel. Mom taught me to figure net, not gross pay. When I borrowed money, she charged me interest—another teaching mechanism.

My parents' life together was smooth on the surface. I never saw them argue, though they did disappear occasionally and sit in the car in the garage, where parlays presumably took place. Suffice it to say that Dad acquiesced and my mother ruled—which was unfortunate. Home life was the American saga, the *I Remember Mama* television show. Or, was it *Leave it to Beaver?*

My parents both finished high school and were products of the Great Depression. Their idea of education for me was being prepared to work.

I regret that they offered so little direction in life, whether in sex education or career guidance. Their world was so small. I also regret not having taken Dad on a vacation with me, because I will never forget the joy he found in reading *National Geographic* and sharing stories about far away places with me. With my beloved sister, Carol, I regret being away the day she died, and cannot forgive myself for her dying alone.

My elementary education after World War II in Dayton was inferior in the sense that Immaculate Conception Grade School ran half days, mornings and afternoons, because of so many children born post war. One group of students went to school from 7 AM to noon, and another group went from 1 PM to 6 PM. The overworked Sisters were grouchy, to say the least.

With my unrecognized dyslexia, school was an intimidating place. I remember when I was in first grade Sister Mary Edmond coming at me and hitting me over the head with the copy of *Little Catholic Messenger* that I was stumbling through. But I did like my second grade teacher, a Sister who volunteered to help me with reading before class began. Along with many other girls, I was fond of a lay teacher who left to get married. We were broken hearted because she was the only lay teacher we had.

My Mom found out that Sister Mary Edmond was making me use my right hand to write or print. Mom then had a meeting with the Principal, Sister Augustine, informing her that I was left-handed and to stop trying to change things!

In the summers, Carol and I would visit Grandma and Grandpa's farm where I remember using boric acid and cotton balls to save baby kitties from eye infections. I swam in the cold, algae-covered milk cooler that was fed by spring water. This was where the milk cans were stored before being trucked away. Today, I still love to swim.

Grandpa drove Carol and I to Richmond, Indiana for Catholic Mass on Sunday. He stayed in the car. Although the visit marked other oddities—like listening to prices of pork bellies on the radio, and like a mouse that ran up my pajama leg while I was sleeping—his not going to Mass is what stayed in my mind.

When we returned home from the summer, I asked Mom why Grandpa didn't go to Mass. Mom simply said theirs was a "different religion," and then my Dad carefully explained that many different faiths are good, and all allow people to go to heaven. What a relief! In childhood, I had been concerned and confused because the Catholic Church taught me that non-Catholic friends were not going to heaven—another assault on my spirit.

Carol and I had wonderful fun-filled memories of our summers on the farm. We loved every minute of it. I'd like to share a few memories with you.

First, I'd like you to picture the 68-acre farm with a circular driveway and large flowering beds in the center. The home was a two-bedroom, wood framed house, with a screened front porch.

Off the porch was the milk cooler, where I swam in the ice cold spring fed water, a back windowed mudroom, and a living room and sitting room where music was played. From the kitchen window, you could see my Grandma's vegetable garden we used for daily meals. She was in charge of the free range chickens, whose home was behind the garden, and to the right was where the pee-pees (baby chickens) lived in a heated, vented structure.

Way in the back of them was a three-seat outhouse with large, medium and small cutout seats. We were instructed to light a wooden match and place it in the hole to make sure there were no snakes at the bottom before we relieved ourselves. When I was about eleven, my Dad, Uncle and Grandpa put in an "in the house outhouse" with a shower. My Grandma, with an embarrassed smile, said she was thrilled,

On the left side of the home was the barn that held my Grandpa's workshop, John Deere tractor, several wagons, a large room for the various animals, the milk house, stalls for animal birthing or sickness, and lastly, the large hay loft.

Let's talk about the animals — one is just as smart as the next one. Old Pet, a sweet, white horse, was the work horse who plowed the truck patch, which was a huge garden planted for canning.

Trixie was frisky, and a fun riding horse, brown in color. There were six to eight dairy cows that needed to be milked twice a day around 6 AM. and 5 PM, seven days a week. My grandparents had to plan their day to be home for every milking.

These cows were amazing. Each one knew which stall was theirs. After they were lined up in the milk house, eating, Grandpa closed their head harness. He always had the radio on. He said it made them relax and milking was easier. When milking was over in the mornings, the cows knew to go out of the barn, down the lane about a half mile to their grazing area, which had shade trees and a spring-fed creek. Grandpa hand milked. Only years later did he have suction cup milkers.

In the side of the milking area, where the feed hay was stored, the cats and kittens would wait for milking to be over. They got fed twice a day in black iron vessels that were about a foot long and six inches deep. My Grandpa would hand us a pail of warm milk that we poured in the feeders, and then broke up white bread. The cats went through around two loaves of bread every three days. This is how Carol and I were able to catch the kittens with eye infections—at the feeder.

The Mary and Billy lambs were next to this building. They were special. They did not catch mice, or give milk. I asked Grandpa what their purpose was and he said, "They are our pets." But, I thought and felt all the animals were our pets, until as an adult, Dad told me the smoke house was also the slaughterhouse, adding, "This is why you kids were not allowed to go into it". To this day, I cannot eat lamb.

Behind the barn there was a large open fenced in area with a six-foot by four-foot watering trough for the livestock. To the left was a fruit orchard, and to the right was the pig house with their watering trough. Across from the pig house was the smoke house.

It seemed like every month a sow was having babies. She was very protective and capable of ramming you, so you never wanted to touch her piglets. They were darling with their tight, curly tails.

There was one rooster, and the free-range chickens knew to go into their nests to lay their eggs. I wonder how Grandma knew which eggs to eat and which eggs were to become pee-pees.

Behind the structures, and down near the cows' grazing area, was where the wheat and hay were planted. During harvest, Carol and I rode in the wagon behind the harvester that shot out wheat. It was cooling to feel the wheat, and grasshoppers, hitting our bodies. We would laugh and laugh.

Also, during harvest, sharecroppers were hired or bartered. Carol and I would help Grandma in the kitchen prepare the meals that were cooked on a black wood stove that we were not to touch. Off the kitchen was a washroom with an old fashioned pump where we got well water. There were about a dozen men gathered around two tables.

My Grandparents both lived to be 86 and died within three months of each other. They ate foods that should have killed them earlier, but they were physically active and ate healthy organic foods and meats.

My Grandma fried chicken with half lard and half butter. She made homemade noodles, mashed potatoes, all kinds of vegetables, bread and cheese. For some reason she always had cheese on the table.

When the dishes were washed and dried, and clean up was finished, Grandma would set the table, placing a white cloth over the table, ready for the next meal. She did this each time the kitchen chores were finished.

My Grandparents gave us chores each summer. We gathered eggs, helped feed the chickens, watered the live stock, cleaned the pee-pee area, gathered garden vegetables, picked fruit from the orchard, and played with the inside and outside dogs.

One morning there was an emergency. My Grandma was on the

black phone (the black phone was one you cranked, the operator came on, and you told her who you wanted to speak to). All I heard was "Come quickly".

We all went to the barn. There was a cow in labor in the horse stall. Neighbor men came in and Grandpa handed them heavy rope. The cow was having difficulty birthing her calf. A rope was tied around the calf's legs, and the men pulled and pulled.

Finally, after about a hundred hours (or it seemed), the calf came out. My Grandpa said I could name it. He said it was a female. I named her Rose Mary. She was a beautiful black and white calf. She had soulful dark brown eyes, and grew into a healthy, sweet, milk cow with babies of her own.

In the evenings, we would wait for the train and wave to the conductor, and he would wave back and blow his horn. We would sit on the screened in porch—my Grandma in her rocker and Grandpa smoking his pipe.

We would watch the lightning bugs and hear the crickets. I don't see lightning bugs any more, nor hear crickets. During the day we would watch the praying mantis. I do not see them either.

Our parents came to the farm every other Saturday because they missed us. This trip was about an hour from Dayton. In the winter, when it was freezing, we all came every Saturday to shovel the poop in the barn. The cows and horses were protected from the freezing weather by being corralled in the barn.

We had to do the shoveling in the afternoon when it was the warmest. The livestock were let out into the pasture so we could clean out the barn and place fresh straw on the floor. The fresh straw was about a foot thick. During the week, Grandpa would shovel up the soiled straw. This cycle continued as long as it was freezing, and the animals could not be outside for long. All the other animals had smaller shelters, which Grandpa could handle by himself.

Mom and Dad's high school graduation photos. Mom's was taken when she was 18, around 1925. Dad was also 18, around 1920.

Above: Dad around 10. (I love this picture!) Left: Mom and Dad. Bottom: Our family around 1974: David, Carol, me, Mom and Dad.

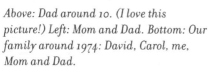

Above: Mom (Right) and
her sister, Lillian, in
the farmhouse kitchen.
Left: Grandmother and
Granddaddy with Mom
(standing) and Lillian.
Below: Grandpa and
Grandma at our home in
Dayton, Ohio.

Left: Dad on riding horse, Trixie. Below Right: Old Pet with a free range chicken. Bottom Left: Carol with a litter of kittens on our grandparents' farm. Bottom Right: Dad on Old Pet a long time ago.

Arizona, 2018.

"IF YOU DON'T LIKE THE ROAD YOU'RE WALKING,
START PAVING ANOTHER."

— DOLLY PARTON

CHAPTER NINE

THE JOURNEY CONTINUES

As I review my childhood, I see female domination as a continuing thread. When I entered my teens, I thought I was claiming independence from my domineering mother, but unconsciously, I was actually substituting another older woman authority figure that exerted a far more dangerous form of control.

Coming from my innocent background, living in a small town with a Roman Catholic family, a matriarchal mother, a "peace at any price" father, and a powerful Catholic Parish Church, I now understand how I fell prey to Sister Rita Celine. I felt I had a religions vocation, and was called by God to join a religious community where I could do good work.

Rita Celine was seeking another victim. She changed my life forever, and I will never know who I might have become had I not been so wounded. I struggle to trust that this was part of a bigger plan, which I am not yet meant to understand—perhaps another lesson in faith.

My family background and sexual abuse in adolescente left me emotionally arrested and unprepared for adulthood. I clearly remained naïve, believing in and trusting the wrong people, and unable to clearly discern reality. Underlying pain and confusion left me searching for something I could not even identify.

In addition to excessive drinking and chronic bouts with depression, my adult life has been marked by another characteristic classic of victims of sexual abuse. My attempts at relationships have veered between celibacy and experiments with pairing.

In the early seventies, when I was a social worker in Dayton, I was introduced to my future husband. We dated for five years and married, which pleased both of our families. However, the relationship did not thrive, and I caused the first divorce in both families.

In 1976, I went to Louisville, Kentucky to graduate school where I received my MSSW. This is when I learned I am dyslexic.

I started therapy again in 1979, feeling unfulfilled in the marriage, depressed, and not understanding why. My husband continued a three-hour commute to where his job was at the time, so we only spent weekends together. This commute probably allowed the marriage to last longer than it should have. Looking back now at the long courtship, and my early need to escape the marriage, I was lost and hungry, seeking something I could not name.

In 1981, I learned that a colleague of mine was a lesbian. Initially, this caused me great anxiety from my own internalized homophobia, but eventually I was able to go and talk to her. In a few months, we began a relationship. During this period, I read everything I could put my hands on about homosexuality and lesbianism, holding a mirror up to myself. Finally, I was beginning to understand what I had been seeking—myself.

My husband was unable to accept that a member of the Roman Catholic Church had sexually abused me, nor could he acknowledge that I was a lesbian. He said nothing. We divorced.

He was a gentle man, extremely hurt by the divorce. He never remarried although. Because I was a lesbian, the Archdiocese of Cincinnati annulled the marriage.

During this period of time, Carol was my support. She accepted my divorce and embraced who I was as a lesbian. Years later, I got the courage to tell Mom I was a lesbian, and she said, "No, you're not." That was the end of any discussion.

In my new lesbian relationship, my partner and I shared raising her daughter until she graduated from high school. Two months after the graduation, my partner informed me that she was either asexual or heterosexual. So after six years we parted, and she subsequently married. This was a difficult time for me. I was devastated, as once again I was losing my family.

One day, I walked into my colleague, OJ's office sobbing. She was a nurse and looked up wide-eyed, holding her breath. Through my tears, I blurted out, "I am a lesbian, and my partner just told me that our relationship is over." OJ's shoulders relaxed as she looked at me and declared, "My God, is that all it is. I thought you were dying of cancer." All things are relative.

OJ and her husband, John, have been dear friends ever since, and have provided much needed acceptance, steadfast support, and love. I am blessed to have them in my life and call them Sister and Brother. We have been friends for 34 years.

Because of the trauma at the end of my lesbian relationship, I needed to focus my energies on a positive outcome. In 1988 I shared with my Mom my desire to buy a building for my private practice. Mom said, "Go for it!" and I did, with her encouragement. Dad had died in 1981, but I know he would have supported this plan also.

In 1992, I began another lesbian relationship, which should have ended quickly, due to our fundamental differences. However, there was an emergency in her family and my partner's grandchild came to live with us between age two to seven.

I remember with fondness fulfilled and classic times with her. We would watch Animal Planet in the mornings waiting for the school bus. One morning birds and ducks were shown, she said, "Aunt Linda, let's watch some fur, I'm tired of feathers."

Another time, she could not decide what she wanted to be when she grew up, so each day for about a week she was a waitress, grocery bag lady, teacher, lawyer, zookeeper, or lifeguard. It was too, too precious.

I love this child to this day and hope our lives intersect in the future. Within the year after she went back to her mother, I ended the relationship. My longing to connect, to belong to a family, and to share my life with someone, marked all my relationships. But, unfortunately, my background led to conflicts springing from dissimilar natures, and an imbalance of independence and control, marring any chances for sustained happiness.

When I look back, the Catholic Church has clearly played a major, but disappointing, role in my life. Time and again, when I have turned to it for answers or comfort, it had its own agenda.

The Catholic Church refuses to seriously address homosexuality in its priesthood or convents and condemns any Catholic homosexual who acts upon his or her sexuality, as this would be "deviant behavior." Using circular reasoning, the Church says not to question it's ever evolving rules, which blocks any educated examination of issues. This dogma, and the pedophile priest cover-up, sent thousands fleeing from the Church. It has failed many, yet paradoxically, within its congregation one finds compassionate members who are congruent in the Church's beliefs, and living out their lives of faith.

In 1990, I returned to the Catholic Church through Dignity, which brings together Catholic gays and lesbians in a worshipping community. The Archdiocese of Cincinnati denied permission to have Mass in its churches, but thankfully, Methodist and Lutheran churches welcomed us. Nearly a decade later, in March of 1999, Cincinnati's Archbishop Daniel Pilarczk began outreach meetings for gays and lesbians; however, we were still barred from having Mass in the Catholic Church.

While I was active in Dignity, I met two important people, Sister Jeannine Gramick, School Sisters of Notre Dame (SND), and Father Robert Nugent, Society D.S., who ministered to the gay and lesbian community for over a quarter of a century. In 1999, Cardinal Joseph Ratzinger, who became Pope Benedict XVI, was Prefect of the Vatican's Congregation for the Doctrine of the Faith. He played a decisive role in writing The Joint Declaration on the Doctrine of Justification issued in 1999, which prevented their work with gays and lesbians from continuing.

Father Bob, stopped his ministry with homosexuals, but Sister Jeannine refused to stop her ministry. She was asked to leave her Religious Order after forty years, but fortunately was offered a home with the Sisters of Loretto. What would Christ say? He who taught the Parable of the Good Samaritan?

Another gay freedom fighter Sister who I found supportive was Sister Joan Chittister, Benedictine Sisters of Erie, Pennsylvania, who wrote a prayer that reads as follows:

Give us the courage to stand with

Our gay and lesbian brothers and sisters,

Their families and those who minister to them.

Give us the grace to confront their rejection,

Whatever its orientation,

Is another manifestation of your goodness.

Give us the vision to recognize and reject

The homophobia around us and in our own hearts, as well.

May we and the church of Jesus open

Our hearts and homes and sanctuaries

To the gay and lesbian community,

To the glory of God they bring in a new voice,

With different face.

Let us bless the God of difference.

Amen

If I have anything to be grateful for from my challenging experiences, it is that they enhanced my personal development. I am exceptionally attuned to women's treatment of other women, and deeply cherish genuine friendship when I discover it.

I have occasionally been baited by acquaintances who say that, since I am a lesbian today, I must have always been a lesbian, and hence Sister Rita Celine must have realized this, making her behavior acceptable. This would be like saying it was appropriate for priests to abuse twelve and thirteen-year-old girls, because they were both heterosexual. Then the worst scenario is paraded before me—that I seduced Rita.

Underlying such homophobic comments are several dubious assumptions: lesbianism, which although it is innate, is also a driving force in the life of a high school sophomore. The young person shrewdly pursues her prey and overcomes the reluctance of a conscientious and innocent adult.

It is embarrassing to pursue this crooked line of inquiry, except to repeat the obvious; I was innocent about any kind of sexuality in the 1950's and 1960's except kissing boyfriends. I did not kiss Rita's cheek, covertly reach for her hand in church, or sneak into bed with her. An experienced seductress, who had twice acknowledged abusing other girls previously, pursued me.

I have struggled for years to forgive Rita and the Sisters of Charity of Cincinnati without completely releasing them from responsibility as faith-filled women of God, ministering to His people through the teachings of Jesus Christ.

As of this writing, they had not done one concrete thing to help victims and survivors of sexual abuse by Religious Women. I believe I forgave Rita when I became an Associate; however, beginning in 2003, when many in the community rejected me again, I was forced to revisit forgiving some of the Sisters of Charity, its President and her Executive Council. This has been a difficult and ongoing journey.

My observations of the leadership of both the Roman Catholic Church and the Sisters of Charity of Cincinnati are that their decisions and policy making are fear driven. *Do nothing that might cause us to lose our comfortable lifestyle, our good image, and our vast accumulated wealth.*

I understand that they are the keepers of Cannon Law, which I am sure for some is a burden. They are also supposed to be the spiritual leaders of their congregation. They should be creating an atmosphere of acceptance and compassion, not rejection and cover-up.

Here lies the dilemma: how to avoid equating forgiveness with letting guilty people remain unaccountable. This is the challenge for all those who begin the journey of forgiveness.

Clinically, I know that being able to forgive empowers and frees me. It allows me to let go of anger, hurt, pain, and rage. I have done everything that I have suggested to clients for years. I made the decision to try to confront my perpetrator in person, and then confront those accountable for her, in person, by telephone and in writing.

However, I made the mistake, not uncommon, of believing that by doing this I would receive a positive response—acknowledgement, ownership, sincere sorrow, and apology for the act of, and cover-up of sexual abuse by a Sister. What I received were continued roadblocks, manipulation, denial, and avoidance.

I will remember the hurt of betrayal, the anger of being ignored and dismissed, and the rage of seduction, but I am no longer feeling it. Years of painful emotional work, the struggle to revisit and write this story, and to give it a public voice, have brought me to a place where I am remembering the past without allowing it to take over my life. I am setting myself free.

In 2006, when I seriously began writing my memoir, I still considered myself a Roman Catholic, although not fully subscribing to all the dogma and politics of the patriarchal church. I was still seeking a home within a Catholic congregation. Now, however, I no longer feel like a Catholic, nor would I seek solace from any organized religion.

In the beginning, I also said that I hoped to gain respect for The Sisters of Charity of Cincinnati. Although I recognize and respect many of the loving Sisters and good works of the Community, sadly, I have not reached a place of respect for the then leadership of the Sisters of Charity of Cincinnati and three other Sisters. I am working at forgiving them.

I see myself clearly as a spiritual person, with a close connection to God, fostered by daily mediation, prayer, spiritual reading, writing in a journal, and interaction with other souls and nature. I am close to God and to my spirit when I hear the rolling surf, feel a cool forest, witness the glory of a crimson sunrise silhouetting a gull in flight, or touch my dog, Maggie May (my fur child), and watch her tail wag. I know Jesus when I look into the eyes of a friend, or the smile of a clerk in the store, and I see the whole tapestry of humankind.

Like all of us, I struggle with my failings and fears, but today my world is full. I have been blessed with good friends, male and female, straight and gay, who accept my complexity that is, after all, part of God's bounty.

Reaching for compassion, love, peace, justice, forgiveness, this is what our lives should be about—The Promised Land of our never-ending spiritual journey.

Abovet:John, me, and OJ in 1994 at my house in Dayton.

Above Right: 1987— OJ and I are hard at work!

Right: OJ on board "Kabuki."

For Linda's birthday,   2-28-97

What can I write that's not yet been said
Through spoken words, gazing eyes, loving touch
Our friendship through these years has indeed been special
In ways we never would have guessed at first meeting
I feel fortunate to have been your friend and confidant
When you first broached some delicate subjects
That were not meant for just anyone to hear
We've had sober discussions, intoxicating playfulness
Wise words shared among friends---our hopes,
Our fears, our dreams, our realities....
Over the years I've come to know that reality is
Very subjective, not empirically defined by any means
What we share in common, what defines us most
Is our very cores, our sentient ways of viewing the world
What I love about you most is your genuine concern
And acceptance of who I am and who I am becoming
With never a judgment or harsh word spoken---
The true caring love of a friend for life

I thank you for who you are, and John thanks you also
(I write for us both) our expression of respect
And hopes that we will remain forever friends

A gift from OJ and John on my 53rd birthday celebration.

Left: Me and OJ celebrating my 70th Birthday at Don Cesar at St. Pete's Beach—February 28, 2014.

Above Right: John and OJ in Arizona, 2018.

Above: Me and OJ at a Helen Reddy concert: "I am Woman!" She wore a flower in her hair.

Right Bottom: a Post-It from OJ after she read the manuscript of this book.

Bravo my friend and sister — this is beautifully written and a story that you need to tell.... Love, OJ
Cinco de Mayo) 5-5-2018

A precious time. The granddaughter of my former partner were very close.

Me and OJ—My dearest friend.

"WHAT I KNOW FOR SURE"

— OPRAH WINFREY

CHAPTER TEN

MEMORIES, SAYING GOODBYE,
AND FORGIVENESS.

*With Chapter 9 completed, I thought I was finished, but I still have
more to say.*

On October 29, 2018, I received a phone call from my dear friend Delia Sizler, Sister of Charity of Cincinnati. Dee informed me that Elizabeth Cashman, Sister of Charity, had died. Her Mass was scheduled for Monday, November 5, 2018 at the Motherhouse.

I was shocked and sad. I thanked Dee for calling and said that I would call her back. I could not continue speaking. When the call came in, I was rereading *The Invention of Wings* by Sue Monk Kidd and felt: "The quiet sat on us like a stone you couldn't lift." (Page 200)

I had to pay my last respects to my friend. Yet by doing so, I had to return to the Motherhouse, and see my home at The Village of Bayley Place. And I had to get on an airplane.

Dee called me two more times concerned about how I was feeling. Finally, on Sunday, I went to my friends' home, and they made flight reservations for Monday. I called Dee, who picked me up at the airport.

It was one of the most difficult trips in my life, and three exceptional caring Sisters of Charity of Cincinnati comforted me.

I was reliving my past during this trip. Suffice to say, I had peace being at the Motherhouse and its holy grounds, yet rage at Barbara Hagedorn, and her Executive Council; two Sisters who held leadership positions, and another Sister.

I told Dee I needed to forgive Barbara Hagedorn. I not only had nightmares of Rita Celine's sexual abuse, but around 2006, I began having interrupted sleep, voiceless, with dreams of being shunned by of Barbara (and her Executive Council not allowing me a collective meeting), and the other three Sisters shunning me. I figured if I forgave Barbara, I could work on forgiving the others.

I also needed to forgive because I was raised by the Roman Catholic Church that to think ill of a priest or Religious Woman was to blaspheme God. (I know, that was then, and this is now, but some things are hard to change or accept.)

I decided to forgive Barbara Hagedorn in writing. When I initially had contacted Barbara by phone in August 2003, she refused to schedule a joint meeting with her Executive Council. She was then President of the Sisters of Charity of Cincinnati. I had to forgive her for this refusal.

I wrote Barbara on January 12, 2019 [See page 197], and I quote the following:

As you may recall. I requested to meet with you and the Executive Council. As you said, "the Council is too busy." so I was left with meeting with you alone. It took a lot of courage for me to meet with you. Had I had the opportunity to meet with the Council, I believe that some or both our pain could have been avoided.

It was important to me to be able to meet with you, as President, and your Leadership Council. It was important because of the positions you held in the SC community. The reason I had wanted to meet with you and the Council in 2003 was because I wanted your witnesses to my voice, to listen to me, and to hear me tell my story of Rita Celine's sexual abuse of me. I feel this was a simple request and your denial of this request has left me to date without a voice, without a told story, and with me being traumatized all over again—because you denied me the opportunity to present my story directly to the Congregational Leadership."

And now I quote from Barbara Hagedorn, Sisters of Charity letter of January 24, 2019 [See page 200] in response to my letter.

After a great deal of prayer and soul searching, I made decisions based on the advice of others—Sisters of Charity Council, the Review Board and consultants involved with sexual abuse allegations—as to how to respond to an allegation of sexual abuse. I feel badly that the process and outcome did not meet your expectations.

Quite honestly, I had to reread the 3rd and 4th paragraphs of my letter several times, thinking I did not make myself clear. But I believe I did, and so did my dearest friend OJ, who said, "Sister Barbara is taking no responsibility for her initial decision to not let you speak with Council. Rather, she kicked her can down the road, or under her rug."

What I know for sure. What God knows for sure, is:

1. I was sexually abused by a sick female religious pedophile, Sister Rita Celine Weadick, SC. I had wondered for years why I put up with her advances for so long. Those who have been abused know why. Each time I was in contact with Rita directly, by phone, notes or letters, I was thrown back to age fifteen and obeyed

her. She had a hold on me being my teacher, and my sponsor for religious life. I held her in esteem.

2. In the early 1980's, I called Rita for a meeting to confront her. The first call, the Sister answering the phone told me, "Sister Rita Celine is not available, and to call back in an hour." When I called back, the person answering the phone said, "This is Sister Marie Karen, Sister Rita Celine is not available, and she will never be available to speak with you."

3. In August 2003, I called Sister Barbara Hagedorn, SC, then President, requesting a joint appointment with her Executive Council. Barbara asked me what was the nature of my request. I said it was personal. Barbara said, "The Council is too busy," and I was left to meet with Barbara by myself in September 2003. Barbara made her decision at our initial phone conversation by not allowing me to speak to the Council. To this day she takes no responsibility for not allowing me to tell my story to her Council.

4. Within a year of my meeting with the President of the Sisters of Charity of Cincinnati, in August 2003, the Sisters living at the Motherhouse were no longer available to go on outings. The Sisters living at Mother Margaret Hall were no longer available to visit with Lucy, my dog, nor me.

5. The Executive Council and various Sisters who held Congregational positions shunned me.

6. Their shunning affected my caring for my Mother, who was then eighty-eight years of age, and in a wheelchair.

7. Because of this toxic environment affecting my care of Mom, I made the painful decision to break the Life Lease contract at the Village of Bayley Place, to the tune of $42,000. I was heartbroken about not keeping my home. I am still heartbroken for I held the

Sisters of Charity of Cincinnati in such high esteem.

8. The Congregational Leadership got what they wanted; my leaving, my moving to another state, my termination of being an Associate of the Sisters of Charity of Cincinnati, my dropping out.

M y truth is setting me free, beginning with Sister Elizabeth Cashman, (AKA Sister John Christopher) agreeing to go to Rita Celine's grave, listening and hearing my voice, and believing that Rita Celine sexually abused me. Elizabeth said, "I believe you and I am sorry." Second, publishing my Memoir is setting me free as it is giving me my voice to be heard and listened to, about my sexual, emotional and spiritual abuse by Sister Rita Celine Weadick.

I am blessed with an Episcopal Church family of Central Florida who are inclusive, grace-filled people, and have programs on social justice and social action. Actually, I am surprised that I have joined an organized Church, however it is an exception to my experiences.

They recently had a workshop on Forgiveness. Forgiveness is a tough one. I had forgiven Rita Celine, which gave me the strength to become an Associate of the Sisters of Charity of Cincinnati, and to return to the Motherhouse.

I had forgiven myself.

I had forgiven Sister Barbara Hagedorn. I am working on forgiving the Council members, the two Sisters in leadership positions, and one other Sister for shunning me.

I daily pray The Our Father, and when it comes to "forgive us our trespasses as we forgive those who trespass against us", I still say this is a tough one. However, I am positive of the outcome as I already have shades of forgiveness.

Thank you for reading my Memoir.

January 12. 2019

Sister Barbara Hagedorn. SC
Sisters of Charity of Cincinnati Motherhouse
5900 Delhi Road
Mount St. Joseph, Ohio 45051

Hello Sister Barbara,

I come in peace and in fairness to me. I write to you. Before I get into the heart of my correspondence with you, let us say a prayer together "Act justly, love tenderly, and walk humbly with your God." Micah 6 8

I want to respond to our meeting in 2003 regarding Rita Celine's sexual abuse of me, and to your letters following my move to Florida.

As you may recall, I requested to meet with you and the Executive Council As you said, "the Council is too busy," so I was left with meeting with you alone. It took a lot of courage for me to meet with you. Had I had the opportunity to meet with the Council, I believe that some of both of our pain could have been avoided.

It was important to me to be able to meet with you, as President, and your Leadership Council It was important because of the positions you held in the SC community The reason I had wanted to meet with you and the Council in 2003 was because I wanted your witnesses to my voice, to listen to me, and to hear me tell my story of Rita Celine's sexual abuse of me. I feel this was a simple request and your denial of this request has left me to date without a voice, without a told story and with me being traumatized all over again – because you denied me the opportunity to present my story directly to the Congregational Leadership.

At this *never happened meeting* with the Council, I had wanted to suggest that the Sisters of Charity of Cincinnati [SC] make a prayer card for those who have been physically or sexually abused, including the emotional and spiritual abuse that follows. God knows even some of your own Sisters have experienced these abuses Secondly, I had wanted to suggest a Day of Recollection for abused persons at the Motherhouse, which remains holy grounds for healing. I made these suggestions in a letter to the Council in 2003, along with a request for a public apology I'm not sure about this request as I tore up my copy of the letter, as I had in the past destroyed Rita Celine's notes to me in the hopes it would relieve THE PAIN

Sister Elizabeth Cashman and I went to Rita Celine's grave. Elizabeth was a witness to my voice, listened, heard my story, and expressed sadness It was a hot and humid day Midway through my story I asked Elizabeth if she was alright, and she said, "I'm fine." A moment of contrast between you and Sister Elizabeth. When I met with you in your office, and told you of Rita Celine s sexual abuse of me, I asked if you were alright. You said, "we are not here to talk about my feelings.

My letter to Barbara Hagedorn, SC, former President of the Sisters of Charity of Cincinnati. The letter is of history and forgiveness. It has taken me 10 years to forgive Barbara.

That same day, I had said to Sister Elizabeth that Rita Celine was a pillar to the Dayton and SC community Sister Elizabeth said, "Rita was never a pillar to the Sisters of Charity In fact, we sent her to alcohol rehab Twice. I think in Michigan and Massachusetts." That day for which I will never forget my gratitude, Elizabeth said, "I believe you," with sorrow

I was joy-filled to become an Associate, live at Bayley Place, walking the holy grounds of the Motherhouse. I truly believe God gave me these gifts to continue to nourish my soul and to be of service to the Sisters of the Motherhouse and to Mother Margaret Hall To have a beautiful peaceful place to care for my Mom in her preparation for her need for a nursing home was a wonderful gift

However, within the year of our meeting, the wagons circled, the shunning began. When I first moved to Bayley Place I would take the Sisters out to eat, to the movies, to the Zoo, visit with them, and listen to their stories. I also took my fur child Lucy, my dog, for a little one-on-one pet therapy when the Sisters would give her treats that they bought. I was honored to bring Holy Communion to the Sisters at Mother Margaret Hall. Soon, the Sisters were not available for outings or visits. What a loss! How would you have felt in this situation?

Although I continued to have Friends of the SC's and Associates visit me, I became isolated. I would be on my back porch, or look out my kitchen window, and across the street were the Congregational Leadership offices where we met. I had to have "custody of the eyes" just to cope in my own home. I felt alone in my grief, despair, and disillusion.

My depression, anxiety, and rage deepened. I was responsible for my Mom. I was losing a grip on caring for her, and I felt a frantic desperation. I had to make the painful decision to get out of this toxic environment and move, giving up on my dream of working on my spiritual life at the Motherhouse. For me, this was the second time I was robbed of my journey

I need to digress – Besides Sister Elizabeth Cashman, I must tell you that Sister Dee Sizler has also been a loyal friend. I remain grateful to her for the faith and grace she has taught me throughout this journey She is a holy woman, having faithfully kept her Professed Vows as had Sister Elizabeth Cashman You might consider praying to these women.

As God is my witness, I know that if it were not for Friends and Associates of the SC s who helped me process my decision, and helped me move, I would not have made it. As importantly these people believed my abuse.

December 2004 I moved to Florida with Mom and Lucy I received my first letter from you dated November 13, 2006, which was in response to my letter dated September 02, 2006, in which you informed me you had shared my letter with your Council (not too busy this time) You stated that your Councils' decision was to have an independent review, and I quote "several religious congregations have formed a Review Board of professionals from various disciplines to review allegations made " I assume this included sexual abuse allegations In this letter you also indicated that you would have someone contact me for an interview

On October 11, 2007 you informed me via letter that Sister Patricia Twohill, a Dominican, would contact me for an interview Sister Patricia and I met on or about March 14 2007 at the Crown Plaza hotel in a conference room in Ft Myers, Florida. Sister Patricia was cordial and courteous. I was frustrated that I had no proof because throughout years of blind rage and despair I tore up or burned proof except for a letter from Rita Celine to my sister, Carol, informing her that Rita Celine would be at the Motherhouse on a day of Family Visitation with the Postulants The letter stated that Carol was not to inform me until Carol met with me. Carol did so informing me I was to meet Rita Celine in a room with a piano on the first floor of the Motherhouse I met with Rita Celine I was shocked at her sexual behavior and the risk it took. I tore up this letter in 2002 in the presence of Sister Elizabeth Cashman out of respect for her believing in me

Out of all of the proof I destroyed, I regret tearing up this letter the most because Carol saved it for 38 years After she died in 2000, I found it in her safe. Carol saved it to help me and I destroyed it – I felt somehow I dishonored her wanting to help me.

At the end of our interview, I asked Sister Patricia if she ever interviewed a person who alleged to have been sexually abused by a religious. She said no. I asked her if she ever interviewed a Lesbian. She said no So much for firsts!

I received your letter dated January 12, 2008 Still not too busy "the Council and I have considered the board's recommendation and have reached our decision based on their recommendation." "Out of pastoral concern for you in your healing process, the Sisters of Charity would offer to pay for six months of counseling or 25 sessions with a licensed therapist/counselor " I am almost 75 years of age, and in my lifetime I never received such a low ball token. As you know I did not respond Even Elizabeth was shocked, and it took a lot to shock her Mea Culpa to you and your Council

I understand that you may have been fearful that I would sue the SC and/or go public with my story The rotten apple that Rita Celine was never caused me to want to harm the SC

I have heard that you have said that you never invited me to Bayley Place. Well my recall is the following   I was sitting in your office showing you swatches of material for furniture I was offering the SC Upon leaving, I asked you what was going on with all of the building across the street You said "oh, that's the Village of Bayley Place – why don't you come?" Perhaps this was an off-the-cuff, casual, no big deal remark from you. The way I experienced this was that we were surrounded by a brilliant light, encircled with peace, and I heard God or the Holy Spirit say, in slow motion, "*why don't you come*" I left your office, went to Bayley Place, and paid my deposit.

You decided what I was to do and I jumped through your hoops I was not even given the courtesy of a copy of any report. Now I'm finished. I have forgiven you but I cannot forget I wish you the best this world has to offer

Sincerely,

Linda S Mahlmeister

5900 Delhi Rd.
Mt. St. Joseph, OH 45051

January 24, 2019

Dear Linda,

Thank you for your letter which I received last week. I wanted to respond with a few thoughts.

No decisions on my part were made with the intention of hurting you. I am really sorry that you were and are experiencing such hurt.

After a great deal of prayer and soul searching, I made decisions based on the advice of others – SC Council, the Review Board and consultants involved with sexual abuse allegations – as to how to respond to an allegation of sexual abuse. I feel badly that the process and outcome did not meet your expectations.

I have prayed for you throughout the years and will continue to do so. May God help us both know greater peace on the path to healing.

In peace,

Barbara

Barbara Hagedorn, SC

The response of Barbara Hagedorn, SC to my letter of forgiveness dated January 12, 2019.

<u>Reclaiming</u>

There's something that's living in the closet.
We all know it. But why was it put there and why has it been kept there?
Some of us have been locked in the closet and are frail from lack of care.
It's gotten crowded, so crowded in fact that the pain of it is forcing the door   open.

    Those outside the closet have more or less denied it exists.
    Those are the busy ones, doing justice and giving charity
        Maybe they pray for the ones locked in,
            those exiled to closet realms.

Inside the closet there is growing rage,
even a spirit of growing rebellion.
A few of the closet dwellers have sneaked out
    to speak what they've experienced.

        Outside, those in denial and fear,
        they want them to keep to themselves.
    They say things like, "Get over it." "Put it behind you."
        And they take a step   away

    The voice of the wounded and closeted rings in the heads of the outside ones.
  Some notice the voices and step forward.
  Some comfort and pity.
Some listen, wanting to accompany this banished life into health and wellness.
Some find in themselves places they've denied and banished.

    Thank you, God, for holding the life we locked away
    Thank you for trusting us now to hold it with you.
  Help us learn how to care, to show hospitality and loving kindness.
    Help us to empathize and connect with our own denied parts.
        Give us compassion.
    May there be no more tolerance for locked closets.
May there be no more giving up opportunities for confessing, for reconciling,
    for experiencing being forgiving and forgiven.

    May the light of your Spirit heal, strengthen and empower us
        individually, as community, as church,
        to be whole and holy.

                  Delia Sizler
                  9/29/04

My friend, Dee, presented this poem to her congregation of Sisters of Charity of Cincinnati.

Me and Dee Sizler, SC, at Clearwater Beach for my 65th birthday, 2009.

Captiva, FL, 2008.

SUNDAY, NOVEMBER 4, 2018 ▌ **THE ENQUIRER** OHIO

Sr. Elizabeth Cashman, S.C.

MOUNT SAINT JOSEPH - Sr. Elizabeth Cashman, S.C., beloved member of the Sisters of Charity, dear sister of the late John Cashman, Mary Weilbacher and Catherine Langen, survived by nieces and nephews. Departed Monday, October 29, 2018 at age 92. The Sisters of Charity and family members will receive guests in the rear of the Motherhouse Chapel at Mount Saint Joseph on Monday, November 5, 2018 from 2 pm until Mass of Christian Burial at 3 pm in the Motherhouse Chapel. Burial will follow in the Motherhouse Cemetery Memorials to the Sisters of Charity Retirement Fund, 5900 Delhi Road, Mount Saint Joseph, OH 45051. Condolences may be expressed at:
GilliganFuneralHomes.com.

Elizabeth's obituary and the prayer at her funeral Mass.

She prayed to take in
all that her heart could hold,
for she so desired to be of one spirit,
one hope, one kindness,
one Essence with all precious others.

God filled her to the brim and she was
faithful forever.

Mass of Christian Burial
Sister Elizabeth Cashman
November 5, 2018

In Loving Memory
of

Sister Elizabeth Cashman

Sister of Charity
Cincinnati, Ohio

Born: October 17, 1926
Entered: September 8, 1945
Died: October 29, 2018

✠

You are my shepherd –
I want nothing more.
You let me lie down in green
meadows, you lead me beside
restful waters; you refresh my soul
You guide me to lush pastures
for the sake of your Name.
Even if I'm surrounded by shadow
of Death, I fear no danger,
for you are with me.
Your rod and your staff--
they give me courage.
You spread a table for me
in the presence of my enemies,
and you anoint my head with oil--
my cup overflows!
Only goodness and love will follow
me all the days of my life,
and I will dwell in your house
for days without end.

PSALM 23

✠

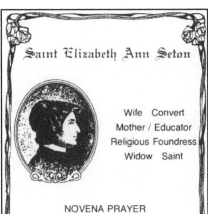

Saint Elizabeth Ann Seton

Wife Convert
Mother / Educator
Religious Foundress
Widow Saint

NOVENA PRAYER

Oh, God our Father glorify here upon earth your servant, St. Elizabeth Ann Seton, by manifesting the power of her intercession through the favor I now implore (*Here mention your intention.*)

We ask this through our Lord Jesus Christ, Your Son, who lives and reigns with You and the Holy Spirit, one God, forever and ever Amen.

Saint Elizabeth Ann Seton was the foundress of the Sisters of Charity of Cincinnati.

ELIZABETH ANN SETON

1774	August 28—Born in New York City
1794	January 25—Married William Seton
1803	December 27—Death of her husband
1805	March 14—Reception into the Catholic Church
	March 25—First Communion
1806	May 26—Confirmation
1808	June 16—Arrival in Baltimore
	September—Opening of the Paca Street School
1809	March 25—Her first vows. Received the title of "Mother"
	June 1—The little band assumes its religious habit
	June 24—Arrival at Emmitsburg, Maryland
	July 31—Community life begins in the Stone House
1810	February 22—Opening of the free school at St. Joseph's
1821	January 4—Death of Mother Seton
1907	Informative Process of Cause begins
1940	February 28—Introduction of Cause at Rome
1959	December 18—Heroicity of virtues declared (Venerable)
1963	March 17—Beatification (Blessed)
1975	September 14—Canonization

NATIONAL SHRINE OF
ST. ELIZABETH ANN SETON
333 South Seton Avenue

a litany of women for the church

Dear God, creator of women in your own image,
born of a woman in the midst of a world half women,
carried by women to mission fields around the globe,
made known by women to all the children of the earth,
give to the women of our time
  the strength to persevere,
  the courage to speak out,
  the faith to believe in you beyond
  all systems and institutions
so that your face on earth may be seen in all its beauty,
so that men and women become whole,
so that the church may be converted to your will
    in everything and in all ways.

We call on the holy women
who went before us,
channels of Your Word
in testaments old and new,
to intercede for us
so that we might be given the grace
to become what they have been
for the honor and glory of God.

Saint Esther, who pleaded against power
  for the liberation of the people,   *--Pray for us.*
Saint Judith, who routed the plans of men
  and saved the community,
Saint Deborah, laywoman and judge, who led
  the people of God,
Saint Elizabeth of Judea, who recognized the value
  of another woman,
Saint Mary Magdalene, minister of Jesus,
  first evangelist of the Christ,
Saint Scholastica, who taught her brother Benedict
  to honor the spirit above the system,

Saint Hildegard, who suffered interdict
  for the doing of right,
Saint Joan of Arc, who put no law above the law of God,
Saint Clare of Assisi, who confronted the pope
  with the image of woman as equal,
Saint Julian of Norwich, who proclaimed for all of us
  the motherhood of God,
Saint Thérèse of Lisieux, who knew the call
  to priesthood in herself,
Saint Catherine of Siena, to whom the pope listened,
Saint Teresa of Avila, who brought women's gifts
  to the reform of the church,
Saint Edith Stein, who brought fearlessness to faith,
Saint Elizabeth Seton, who broke down boundaries
  between lay women and religious
  by wedding motherhood and religious life,
Saint Dorothy Day, who led the church
  to a new sense of justice,

* * *

Mary, mother of Jesus,
  who heard the call of God and answered,
Mary, mother of Jesus,
  who drew strength from the woman Elizabeth,
Mary, mother of Jesus,
  who underwent hardship bearing Christ,
Mary, mother of Jesus, who ministered at Cana,
Mary, mother of Jesus, inspirited at Pentecost,
Mary, mother of Jesus, who turned the Spirit of God
  into the body and blood of Christ, pray for us. Amen.

Benedictine Sisters of Erie, PA
Text by Joan Chittister, OSB / Image by Peter Wm. Gray, SS

Benetvision
355 East Ninth Street • Erie, PA 16503-1107
Phone (814)459-5994 • Fax (814)459-8066

Cost per 100 cards $9.00 (includes postage & handling)

I HAVE A HEALTHY, FULFILLING SPIRITUAL LIFE, GUIDED BY WORDS
THAT I QUOTE FROM DESIDERATA:

Go placidly amid the noise and haste, and remember what peace

there may be in silence. As far as possible without surrender be on

good terms with all persons. Speak your truth quietly and clearly, and

listen to others, even the dull and ignorant, they, too, have their story.

Avoid loud and aggressive persons, they are vexations to the spirit. If

you compare yourself with others, you may become vain and bitter;

for always there will be greater and lesser persons than yourself. Enjoy

your achievements as well as your plans. Keep interested in your own

career, however humble; it is a real passion in the changing fortunes of

time. Exercise caution in your business affairs; for the world is full of

trickery. But let this not blind you to what virtue there is; many persons

strive for high ideals; and everywhere life is full of heroism.

Be yourself, especially, do not feign affection. Neither be cynical about love; for in the face of aridity and disenchantment it is perennial as the grass. Take kindly the counsel of the years, gracefully surrendering the things of youth. Nurture strength of spirit to shield you in sudden misfortune. But do not distress yourself with imaginings. Many fears are born of fatigue and loneliness. Beyond a wholesome discipline, be gentle with yourself. You are a child of the universe, no less than the trees and the stars; you have a right to be here. And whether or not it is clear to you, no doubt the universe is unfolding as it should. Therefore be at peace with God, whatever you conceive him to be, and whatever your labors and aspirations, in the noisy confusion of life, keep peace with your soul. With all its sham, drudgery and broken dreams, it is still a beautiful world. Be careful. Strive to be happy.   Author unknown.

Peace Prayer of St. Francis

Lord, make me an instrument of your peace;
where there is hatred, let me sow love;
where there is injury, pardon,
where there is doubt, faith,
where there is despair, hope;
where there is darkness, light;
and where there is sadness, joy;

Grant that I may not so much seek
to be consoled as to console;
to be understood, as to understand,
to be loved as to love;
for it is in giving that we receive,
it is in pardoning that we are pardoned,
and it is in dying that we are born to eternal life.

Two of my favorite prayers.

MY LORD GOD,
*I have no idea where I am
going I do not see the road ahead
of me. I cannot know for certain
where it will end. Nor do I really
know myself, and the fact that I
think that I am following your will
does not mean that I am actually
doing so. But I believe that the desire to please you does in fact
please you. And I hope I have that
desire in all that I am doing I hope
that I will never do anything apart
from that desire. And I know that
if I do this you will lead me by the
right road though I may know nothing about it. Therefore will I trust
you always though I may seem to
be lost and in the shadow of death.
I will not fear, for you are ever
with me, and you will never leave
me to face my perils alone.* ✝✝✝

THOMAS MERTON
— *Thoughts in Solitude*

(C) Abbey of Gethsemani

Me and my dearest friend, OJ.

ACKNOWLEDGMENTS

OJ and John – Thank you for your loyal friendship, for being my Sister and Brother and loving and believing in me.

Toots – Thank you for encouraging me.

Dee – Thank you for your passionate advocacy in believing me about my abuse by one of your own, for your spiritual Sisterhood and letter of support.

Mary and Diana – Thank you for your letters of support to Barbara Hagedorn, SC, then President of the Sisters of Charity of Cincinnati.

Betsy and Lori – Thank you for your unyielding support and encouragement.

Father John – Thank you for your spiritual approval and the go-ahead.

Brenda – Thank you for typing my memoir.

John and Wendy – Thank you for typing, proofing and helping me get my Memoir published.

Made in the USA
Middletown, DE
20 July 2019